THE MYTH OF BLACK PROGRESS

The myth of black progress

ALPHONSO PINKNEY

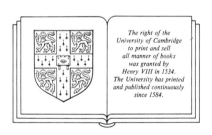

The right of the
University of Cambridge
to print and sell
all manner of books
was granted by
Henry VIII in 1534.
The University has printed
and published continuously
since 1584.

CAMBRIDGE UNIVERSITY PRESS

CAMBRIDGE

LONDON   NEW YORK   NEW ROCHELLE

MELBOURNE   SYDNEY

Published by the Press Syndicate of the University of Cambridge
The Pitt Building, Trumpington Street, Cambridge CB2 1RP
32 East 57th Street, New York, NY 10022, USA
296 Beaconsfield Parade, Middle Park, Melbourne 3206, Australia

© Cambridge University Press 1984

First published 1984

Printed in the United States of America

Library of Congress Cataloging in Publication Data
Pinkney, Alphonso.
The myth of black progress.
Includes bibliographical references and index.
1. Afro-Americans–Economic conditions. 2. Afro-
Americans–Social conditions–1975– . 3. Afro-
Americans–Civil rights. 4. Discrimination in educa-
tion–United States. I. Title.
E185.8.P56 1984   305.8′96073 84–1912
ISBN 0 521 25983 5

To the members of the underclass,
citizens in the society but not a part of it

CONTENTS

Contents

PREFACE

REPORTS of the ongoing oppression of Afro-Americans are commonplace: In 1983 a five-year-old black child was murdered in California by a white police officer who claimed that the child had a handgun; four blacks were indiscriminately killed by New Orleans police following the murder of a white police officer; a black transit worker was killed by a white mob in Brooklyn as he stopped with co-workers in a delicatessen for food; white voters refused to support well-qualified black candidates; the black candidate for mayor of Chicago, along with a Democratic candidate for president, was refused permission to speak by a crowd of white racists at a Roman Catholic church on Palm Sunday; spokespersons for the administration continued to take positions opposed to the aspirations of blacks; twice as many black adults were unemployed as whites and among teenagers it was three blacks for every white; Little Rock resegregated its schools because of white boycotts.

At the same time we are bombarded with books and articles, by blacks and whites, claiming that in this country race is no longer a salient variable in relations between blacks and whites. These writers have given support to the conservative trend in the United States. Some of them hold important positions in the administration and others are courted by government policy makers. These people continue to hold fast to their ahistorical positions in the face of the continuing oppression of black people. While their motives are difficult to fathom their positions no doubt fuel the antiblack feelings of conservatives, in and out of government. And, equally crucial, in many instances their pronouncements directly contradict the data gathered by government agencies.

Preface

This book is an effort to present a different assessment of the status of black Americans. It takes the position that although racism in the United States is less pronounced and racists are less vocal and overt since the Civil Rights Act of 1964, race continues to be an ever-present part of the American way of life.

In 1978 several black sociologists met in San Francisco and expressed their outrage at this conservative trend. It was their fear that government policy makers would seize on these pronouncements to discontinue such programs as affirmative action, busing, and others specifically designed to, in part, make amends for past injustices to black people. Several expressed the hope that someone would come forth and present what they considered to be a more objective exegesis of the black population in the United States.

The present work is not meant to be a specific corrective to the writings of conservatives; rather, it attempts to evaluate the current status of Afro-Americans in the United States in comparison to that of whites. In doing so it is hoped that a more accurate analysis of the state of black America will result.

Walter Stafford is responsible for Chapter II, "Economic decline and the rise of the new conservatism"; in addition, he is responsible for a section of Chapter VII, "And the black underclass." As is their custom, my editor, Liz Maguire, and others at Cambridge University Press have been both helpful and cooperative.

New York City   Alphonso Pinkney
1984

I

INTRODUCTION: THE PERSISTENCE OF RACISM IN THE UNITED STATES

IT is ironic that at a time when there appeared to be some minor progress in improving the citizenship status of black people in the United States, and some official commitment to racial equality, the national mood shifted rather abruptly to one of continued subjugation and racial oppression. Beginning with the *Brown v. Board of Education* decision of the Supreme Court in 1954 and continuing through most of the decade of the 1960s, there was reason for America's black citizens to suspect that their liberation from oppression was underway and that those citizens opposed to equality for blacks were in a small minority. And it appeared that government agencies supported their aspirations. But as is so characteristic of American society, the national mood shifted radically, and through a variety of actions at all levels, blacks found themselves with fewer allies in their quest for equality. Public support for black progress virtually disappeared, and blacks were once again being blamed for their plight in a society where racism has historically been an integral part of all of its institutions and has served to maintain and protect white privilege. How is it possible that after a few years of apparent commitment to full equality for black people, the mood of the American people could shift so drastically?

Clearly there are many answers to this question, but of special relevance to the present work is the confusion between equality in principle and equality in practice. Social scientists, government officials, and the general public have tended to assume, however naively, that the legislative and judicial acts on behalf of America's black colony between 1954 and 1968, which served to elevate the citizenship status of black people to that of white people, thereby accomplishing

1

equality in principle, would lead to immediate equality in practice. Such was not the case.

It is undeniable that some progress toward eliminating discriminatory barriers against blacks was achieved in the last half of the 1950s and the decade of the 1960s, but these actions failed largely because racial discrimination is deeply rooted in the structure of American institutions. In many cases, those in power in these institutions profit from the maintenance of racial discrimination, for it is to their economic advantage. When a law is enacted, for example, those entrusted with its enforcement usually have available to them a variety of means for evading it with impunity. And it is frequently the responsibility of the victims to prove the case against wealthy corporations with unlimited funds for legal expenses. Consequently, the long-standing problems of poverty, unemployment, job discrimination, inadequate housing, and barriers to education continue to reinforce the subordinate position of Afro-Americans. Deeply ingrained white racism serves to justify the oppression of blacks.

In the fourteen years between 1954 and 1968, no fewer than six major legislative and judicial acts geared toward elevating the citizenship status of Afro-Americans became part of American law. The *Brown* decision is widely considered to have been the first major victory against racial segregation and discrimination in the twentieth century. The Supreme Court ruled, without dissent, that the segregation of children in public schools solely on the basis of race deprives them of equal educational opportunities. Furthermore, the Court ruled that the segregation of students on the basis of race "generates a feeling of inferiority as to their status in the community that may affect their hearts and minds in a way unlikely ever to be undone." Finally, the Court held that racially segregated public education deprives those students who are segregated of the equal protection laws guaranteed by the Fourteenth Amendment.

Those states maintaining official segregation based on race engaged in "massive resistance" campaigns, aimed at maintaining separate public schools for blacks and whites. So successful were these campaigns that ten years after the original decision, only about 1 percent of all black pupils enrolled in

2

public schools in the eleven states of the original Confederacy were attending integrated schools, and many of these students were forced to attend segregated classes within these schools. The greatest impetus to school desegregation in the South occurred ten years after the 1954 decision, as a result of the Civil Rights Act of 1964, which authorized the Department of Health, Education, and Welfare (HEW) to withhold federal funds from school districts maintaining segregated schools. Although HEW has been timid in enforcing the law (Title VI), twenty years after the *Brown* decision school districts in the South had made substantial progress in eliminating segregated schools in that region. The same could not be said of the desegregation of school staffs, however. The U.S. Commission on Civil Rights, in a report, *Twenty Years After Brown: Equality of Educational Opportunity*, pointed out that the desegregation of dual systems in the South had led to the displacement or demotion of black school staff and that few school systems employed black administrators.[1]

In addition to racial discrimination in education, there were other acts designed to improve the status of American blacks. Perhaps one of the most difficult areas for blacks historically has been the right to vote, one of the basic rights ostensibly guaranteed to all citizens by the Constitution. Immediately following the Civil War, two amendments, the Fourteenth and Fifteenth, were ratified to protect the voting rights of the newly freed slaves. Additional laws were enacted during Reconstruction, but all of these were insufficient to insure this basic right. Therefore, Congress passed the Civil Rights Act of 1957, which attempted to guarantee that any black person in the South desiring to vote could do so. The federal government, through the Department of Justice, was empowered to initiate lawsuits to ensure blacks the right to vote in federal, state, and local elections. Because this law failed to achieve its aim, Congress enacted the Civil Rights Act of 1960, which empowered the attorney general to certify blacks as qualified voters in areas where they had been kept from voting through acts of discrimination. This act required that registration forms, applications, and other records be kept for a specified time, and it also empowered federal courts to appoint referees to ensure that all qualified applicants wishing to vote could do so. Although this act permitted a few southern black citizens to register to vote, the number added to the voting rolls was minuscule.

Although the *Brown* decision was the most far-reaching federal act in support of black people in the twentieth century, it had little effect on the millions of blacks facing daily segregation and discrimination in all institutions in American life. Throughout most of the society blacks were legally relegated to the status of second-class citizens. The atrocities they faced in the South during the civil rights movement alerted the remainder of the nation and the world to their plight. And the massive March on Washington in 1963 gave added impetus to the passage of the Civil Rights Act of 1964, by far the most comprehensive piece of legislation affecting black rights in this century.

This act covered virtually all areas of American life and addressed itself to both de facto and de jure segregation and discrimination. The major provisions of this act are (1) sixth-grade education was established as a presumption of literacy for voting purposes; (2) segregation and discrimination in places of public accommodation (hotels, motels, restaurants, etc.) were outlawed; (3) public facilities (parks, swimming pools, stadiums, etc.) were desegregated; (4) the attorney general was authorized to file desegregation suits; (5) discrimination was outlawed in federally assisted activities; (6) virtually all discrimination by all employers and unions was outlawed; (7) the attorney general was authorized to intervene in suits in which persons alleged denial of equal protection of laws under the Fourteenth Amendment. Of crucial importance for black people, the Civil Rights Act of 1964 authorizes federal financial and technical aid to assist school districts with desegregation and directs federal agencies to withhold federal funds from state and local agencies that fail to comply with the law.

It might be said then that the Civil Rights Act of 1964 abolished virtually all forms of segregation and discrimination against black people that had been the cornerstone of American race relations for centuries. And although the provisions of this act contained enforcement mechanisms, those agencies and individuals charged with enforcing the law were less

4

than diligent in their mandate. Consequently, it became necessary to enact additional civil rights legislation. For example, although several pieces of legislation (including the 1964 act) addressed the problem of voting rights for black people, as late as 1965 discrimination in registration and voting continued on a wide scale, particularly in the South. Therefore, the Voting Rights Act of 1965 was enacted to finally enfranchise Afro-Americans living in the South.

The Voting Rights Act of 1965 resulted from continued refusal of Southern white officials to permit blacks to exercise a right that had ostensibly been guaranteed by the Fifteenth Amendment of 1870. At the urging of officials of the Department of Justice, civil rights leaders decided to focus their attention on the state of Alabama, one of the most intransigent with regard to black voting. When attempts to register blacks to vote met with resistance from state officials, a massive march from Selma to Montgomery was planned in the spring of 1965. Local law enforcement officials prohibited the march for several days, and when permission to march was finally granted, violence was unleashed by whites, resulting in three deaths and scores of injuries. Later that year Congress passed the Voting Rights Act of 1965, which actually allowed blacks in the South to register and vote, many for the first time. Literacy tests and other devices previously employed to disfranchise them were eliminated. In addition, one provision authorized federal officials to supervise the registration of blacks in political subdivisions where discrimination had been practiced. Blacks in the South were finally permitted to register and vote some ninety-five years after ratification of the Fifteenth Amendment.

Adequate housing has always been a major problem facing black Americans; most have been too poor to secure satisfactory housing, and the minority who could afford adequate housing of their choice were most often victims of segregation and discrimination. For several years fair housing legislation was introduced in Congress but was defeated. Then when civil rights leaders attempted to break the segregated housing barriers in Chicago and several other cities, angry whites resorted to violence. After the assassination of Martin Luther King, Jr., in 1968, Congress enacted the Civil Rights Act of

1968, a major part of which deals with discrimination in housing. Among other things, this act prohibits discrimination in selling or renting most housing in the United States. The right to housing on a nondiscriminatory basis was the last of the basic rights to be secured by black people, and it must be added that it is also the area in which the law is most often evaded and least often enforced.

In the period of 1954–78 many laws were enacted to elevate the citizenship status of black Americans, and though they might have equalized the rights of blacks in the South with those in other parts of the country, those laws in practice have meant minimal gains for America's 25 million black citizens. And as Chapters 5–8 indicate, the gap between blacks and whites in the economic sphere has indeed widened rather than narrowed. And there is good reason to speculate that the growing conservatism of the 1970s and 1980s is partially responsible for the discrepancy between black equality in principle and in practice.

The situation at present is painfully reminiscent of what happened to black people after the Civil War. The abolitionists assumed that the end of slavery meant equality for the newly freed blacks. Their task had been completed, they felt, and most of them turned their interest to other areas. After Reconstruction many whites outside the South who had initially opposed slavery and supported the cause of blacks, ultimately adopted the southern view of race relations, assuming that blacks had been responsible for the failure of Reconstruction. Several "liberal" publications such as *Atlantic Monthly, Harper's Weekly,* and *The Nation* carried articles charging that blacks were innately inferior to whites (scientific racism) and that they were incapable of participating in the white people's civilization. For black people this was a critical time. Segregation and discrimination became institutionalized before the end of the nineteenth century and remained an integral part of the "American way of life" throughout the first half of the twentieth century.

History has a way of repeating itself, but the recent spread of black consciousness is so pervasive and so profound that no matter how hard the conservatives try, they are not likely to win this one.

SOCIAL SCIENTISTS AND THE MYTH OF BLACK PROGRESS

Several works have appeared in recent years by sociologists and other social scientists alleging that race is no longer an important variable in American society. Others have maintained that black Americans of comparable educational achievement have reached income parity with white Americans. There are even those who maintain that black people in the United States now enjoy some advantages over white people, particularly in education and employment, and that more than half of all black families have achieved middle-class status. Some claim that affirmative action programs have served to close the income gap between black and white Americans, and that legislative acts and court decisions of the 1960s and 1970s have transformed American society into an egalitarian one in practice as well as in principle.

It is the contention here that these works put forth major myths regarding race relations in the United States. They present an erroneous picture of the status of black people, and all too often influence public policy ostensibly aimed at alleviating problems and powerlessness among Afro-Americans and other people of color. When not making exaggerated claims on the question of black progress, these social scientists tend to blame Afro-Americans (the victims) for their lack of progress rather than the forces in the society that serve to maintain their oppression (the perpetrators).

As early as 1965, for example, the Office of Policy Planning and Research of the Department of Labor issued a controversial report, compiled by Daniel Moynihan, entitled *The Negro Family: The Case for National Action.*[2] In this report Moynihan declared: "At the heart of the deterioration of the fabric of Negro society is the deterioration of the Negro family. It is the fundamental source of weakness in the Negro family at the present time."[3] Moynihan attempted to support this allegation by using such indicators as the high dissolution rate of urban black marriages and the high proportion of black families headed by females and by stating that the "breakdown" of black families had led to a "startling increase in welfare dependency." On the basis of these charges,

7

Moynihan characterized the black family as a "tangle of pathology."

In June of 1965 President Lyndon Johnson announced in a commencement address at Howard University that he would convene in the fall " a White House conference of scholars and experts, and outstanding Negro Leaders – men of both races – and officials of government at every level." That he was influenced by Moynihan (who assisted in drafting the speech) was made evident when he declared: "The family is the cornerstone of our society. . . When the family collapses it is the children that are usually damaged. When this happens on a massive scale the community itself is crippled."[4] Angered by the age-old American tactic of "blaming the victim," black civil rights leaders and educators forced the scaling down of the White House Conference to a planning meeting for a larger one to be held the following spring. When the conference finally met, those in attendance seized the opportunity to criticize what had become known as the Moynihan Report. And an anthology of responses to his assertions was subsequently compiled.[5]

Five years after the publication of the report, Moynihan, who had become counselor to President Richard Nixon, issued his now infamous "benign neglect" memorandum.[6] He said that "the time may have come when the issue of race could benefit from a period of 'benign neglect.' The subject has been too much talked about. The forum has been too much taken over by hysterics, paranoids, and boodlers on all sides." He continued: "We may need a period in which Negro progress continues and racial rhetoric fades. . . Greater attention to Indians, Mexican-Americans and Puerto Ricans would be useful." This recommendation was made because "in quantitative terms, which are reliable, the American Negro is making extraordinary progress." Regarding the economic status of blacks, he reported that "young Negro families are achieving income parity with young white families. Outside the South, young husband-wife Negro families have 99 percent the income of whites."

What Moynihan failed to mention, however, is that such families comprise a small fraction (approximately 10 percent) of all black families. The remaining 90 percent lags far behind white families in income.

Social scientists and the myth of black progress

In the early 1960s Moynihan coauthored a book with Nathan Glazer. Glazer wrote the chapter on blacks, in which he had this to say: "It is not possible for Negroes to view themselves as other ethnic groups viewed themselves because – and this is the key to much in the Negro world – the Negro is only an American, and nothing else. He has no values and culture to guard and protect."[7] Such a comment is so absurd that further comment on it would only serve to dignify it.

Since that time Glazer has written extensively about blacks, usually in a degrading manner. For example, in his *Affirmative Discrimination,* he blames blacks for their economic plight. In his view much of black unemployment stems, not from the scarcity of jobs or employment discrimination, but from "the alternative attractions of welfare" and the refusal of young blacks to accept available jobs because of the attraction of "illicit activities."[8] He is strongly opposed to affirmative action in employment, education, and housing. He supports the racist Boston School Committee, which made it difficult and often impossible for black children to attend school. He constantly refers to blacks as "criminally inclined" and "killers of unoffending shopkeepers." The black community is seen as a tangle of pathology. It is no wonder that he finds it necessary to constantly remind his readers that he is opposed to discrimination.

He is, of course, opposed to compensation for past injustices and maintains that public policy should be based on "individual freedom," which seems somewhat naive given that race continues to be one of the most crucial variables in American society. Finally, it is simply incorrect to maintain, as Glazer does, that historically in the United States "the group characteristics of an individual were of no concern to government."

Ben Wattenberg and Richard Scammon, two social scientists, reported in 1973 that a "revolutionary" development had taken place in the United States in the preceding dozen years: "For the first time in the history of the republic, truly large and growing numbers of American blacks have been moving into the middle class, so that by now these numbers can reasonably be said to add up to a *majority* of black Americans – a slender majority, but a majority nevertheless."[9] In fact, the proportion of middle-income black families has not increased

9

significantly in recent years, and indeed it is far less than one-half of the total.[10]

According to data from the Bureau of Labor Statistics, approximately 23 percent of all black families in 1975 were middle-income.[11] This represented a 3 percent decline from 1972. Part of the difficulty in such discussions stems from the varying definitions of middle class. Wattenberg and Scammon rely more heavily on occupational status than on income. For example, their definition of middle class for blacks includes "plasterers, painters, bus drivers, lathe operators, secretaries, bank tellers, and automobile assembly-line workers." In short, they simply and conveniently define the concept to support their erroneous position.

In 1974 two cliometricians, or economic historians who apply quantitative methods to the study of history, published a two-volume work, *Time on the Cross,* with the subtitle *The Economics of American Negro Slavery.*[12] This work received widespread media coverage and mixed reviews.[13] It was severely criticized by black scholars, but some white scholars considered it to be an important work on slavery. For example, Nathan Glazer described the work as "quality scholarship" that adds to "historical truth."

According to Fogel and Engerman slavery was a benign institution. This is in striking contrast to the works of other social scientists as well as conditions reported in slave narratives. They feel that the application of quantitative methods to the study of history makes for greater reliability of findings. Accusing traditional historians of using "fragmentary" and "impressionistic" (i.e., unscientific) data, they, assisted by high-speed computers, present elaborate mathematical equations, graphs, and tables to introduce several "principal corrections" to traditional notions about slavery.

Time on the Cross is a strange book, one that does little to advance our understanding of slavery in the United States. The authors themselves use "fragmentary" and "impressionistic" data when it serves their purpose. And they arrive at questionable assumptions; for example, one wonders why so many other historians (black and white) were in error about life under slavery, and how so many slaves were unaware of the affection of slaveholders for them. We are told by the computer that slave breeding was a myth; that "most planters shunned direct interference in the sexual practices of slaves." The black "family" in slavery was the basic unit of social organization. Black women were rarely exploited sexually by slaveholders, and families were almost never destroyed by the sale of one of the partners. Expectant and new mothers were given such special care that the Fogel-Engerman description sounds like the treatment accorded pregnant women and new mothers in socialist countries and in advanced welfare-state capitalist countries.

Fogel and Engerman maintain that food, shelter, and clothing allocations were generous during slavery, and the slave cabins are referred to as "cottages." Health care for slaves was of high quality as is illustrated by the low illness rate among them; the average slave missed only twelve days' work per year. Could it have been that they were required to work even when ill? They maintain that the life expectancy of slaves was 12 percent below that of white Americans, but about the same as that of people in France and Holland (whatever that means, for they were in the United States, not Europe).

Prior to the advent of the cliometric revolution, historians had led us to believe that slaves were a troublesome property, and that consequently, punishment, especially whipping, was widespread. Fogel and Engerman admit that whipping was part of the system of punishment and rewards, but they minimize its frequency and severity because they maintain that most slaveholders were not sadistic.

Finally, Fogel and Engerman, in their apology for slavery in the United States, do not address themselves to some basic questions. If slavery was a benign institution, why did the slaves pose so many problems for slaveholders? Why did so many escape? Why the enactment of the fugitive slave laws? What about the documented revolts? And the acts of sabotage? *Time on the Cross* presents an unfair interpretation of one of history's harshest systems of social relations.

Thomas Sowell, a black economist, opposes affirmative action in employment (especially in colleges and universities), preferential admissions to college, and public school busing. His opposition to preferential treatment as a means of making amends for past injustices rests on two assumptions: that public opinion polls indicate that minorities themselves oppose such treatment, and that the income of black workers reached its peak before the onset of affirmative action programs and has declined since.[14] The first assumption is a strange one because special preferences for various groups in the society are commonplace, and the recipients of these benefits have never been asked how they felt about them; they simply take them for granted. There are special preferences for veterans and for the handicapped, to name but two groups. To deny such preferences to the victims of centuries of oppression by the society can only be considered a gross act of cruelty.

Sowell's second assumption is even stranger because he condemns affirmative action programs in principle, while at the same time he blames such programs for the widening income gap between black and white workers. Lack of enforcement of the law is not even considered. Furthermore, he rejects the notion that such programs are necessary for professional schools in order to supply doctors and lawyers for black neighborhoods. He assumes, quite in error, that white professionals are as likely to practice in the black community as black professionals. It is undeniable that minority communities have low ratios of doctors and lawyers. His general position is that "the past is a great unchangeable fact. *Nothing* is going to undo its sufferings and injustices, whatever their magnitude."[15] This statement misses the whole point of affirmative action programs. Their function is not to change history, but rather to make amends for past injustices. But Sowell's conservative bias is so strong that he sometimes shows a lack of understanding of human character. He writes: "Once personal choice becomes a mere inconvenience to be brushed aside by bureaucrats or judges, something precious will have been lost by all people from all backgrounds."[16] What meaningful choice have black people ever had in the United States?

Like other conservative social scientists, Sowell insists that income parity has been achieved by college-educated black males outside the South. Even if this were true, which it is not, he is referring to a minute fraction of blacks in the United States. Rather than proving his point, he simply resorts to relying on the faulty data provided by Wattenberg and Scammon.

Still another economist, Richard Freeman, emphasizes the progress that some black workers have made without considering the enormous gap that remains between black and white earnings.[17] He characterizes blacks between twenty-five and thirty-five years of age as a "black elite." He maintains that class differences are becoming more important among blacks, most notably the relationship between family background and occupational success. Family background, he maintains, is particularly important in terms of the probability of professional-managerial job attainment by black males.

The major problem with Freeman's analysis and that of others is the measurement process. It is accurate that younger blacks moved into higher-status occupations in the late 1960s. However, by not identifying types of employment sectors and providing comparisons with white males and the structure of the occupational groupings, a misleading interpretation of progress is provided. Specifically, by employing occupational categories utilized by the Bureau of Labor statistics, Freeman shows by comparing entering black workers (twenty-five to thirty-four years of age) with retiring workers (fifty-five to sixty-four years of age) that significant numbers of blacks moved from lower-level to upper-level occupations between 1960 and 1970.

One of the more recent works to paint an erroneous picture of the plight of Afro-Americans is William Wilson's *The Declining Significance of Race: Blacks and Changing American Institutions*.[18] The general point made by Wilson is that for the first time in American history class is more important than race in determining access to privilege and power. Specifically, Wilson sets forth his thesis in the opening sentence of the first chapter of the book: "Race relations in America have undergone fundamental changes in recent years, so much so that now the life chances of individual blacks have more to do with their economic class position than with their day-to-day encounters with whites."[19] There are so many faulty (even naive) interpretations in this short book that it is an amazing piece of work coming from a black sociologist. In the first

13

place, there is evidence that the economic gap between black and white workers is widening rather than narrowing, and discrimination against blacks, regardless of class, continues to be widespread.

Yet Wilson makes statements that are not fully supported that most blacks in the United States could only find shocking. A few examples: "In short, unlike previous periods of American race relations, economic class is now a more important factor than race in determining job placement for blacks."[20] "It is also the case that class has become more important in determining black life-chances in the modern industrial period."[21] "Talented and educated blacks are experiencing unprecedented job opportunities in the growing government and corporate sectors, opportunities that are *at least* comparable to those of whites with equivalent qualifications."[22] "The recent mobility patterns of blacks lend strong support to the view that economic class is clearly more important than race in predetermining job place and occupational mobility."[23] Finally, "Despite the fact that the recession of the early 1970s decreased job prospects for all educated workers, the more educated blacks continue to experience a faster rate of job advancement than their white counterparts."[24]

Rather than deal at length with Wilson's statements here, it is important to note that the Association of Black Sociologists, at its annual meeting in San Francisco in September 1978, passed a resolution critical of Wilson's book.

> The Association of Black Sociologists is concerned that the book by Professor William Julius Wilson entitled *The Declining Significance of Race* was considered sufficiently factual to merit the Spivack award from the American Sociological Association.
>
> The book clearly omits significant data regarding the continuing discrimination against blacks at all class levels. It misinterprets even facts presented in the volume, and draws inferences that are contrary to the conclusions that other black and white scholars have reached with reference to the salience of race as a critical variable in American society.
>
> It is the consensus of this organization that this book denies the overwhelming evidence regarding the significance of race and the literature that speaks to the contrary.
>
> We certainly do not deny the freedom of any scholar to pub-

lish his or her work. However, it is the position of this organization that the sudden national attention given to Professor Wilson's book obscures the problem of the persistent oppression of blacks. There is an abundance of evidence that documents the significance of race as a critical variable in the denial of opportunities for blacks. For example, the United States Department of Housing and Urban Development has recently published a study which systematically and carefully documents that blacks of all social classes experience pervasive discrimination. Even within the discipline of sociology discrimination has been rampant. In the seventy-three year history of the American Sociological Association only one black person has been elected president, and that was more than three decades ago.

In the past reactionary groups have seized upon inappropriate analyses as a basis for the further suppression of blacks. We would hope that this is not the intent of the recent recognition that has been given to Professor Wilson's book. It must be underscored that the life chances of blacks (e.g., employment, housing, health care, education, etc.) are shocking and that discrimination in some areas is so pervasive that the income and employment gaps between blacks and whites have widened.

The Association of Black Sociologists is outraged over the misrepresentation of the black experience. We are also extremely disturbed over the policy implications that may derive from this work and that, given the nature of American society, are likely to set in motion equally objectionable trends in funding, research and training.

As a sociologist Wilson should understand that he is writing about a very small fraction of black people, and that even in this case, it is impossible to separate one aspect of society (employment) from the many institutions that continue to discriminate against people of color. For example, there is every reason to believe that the best-educated and most economically mobile blacks have as much difficulty in obtaining housing in most sections of the country as their low-income fellow blacks.

Finally, it is important to note the revival of scientific racism in America. This revival was initiated by an educational psychologist, Arthur Jensen, who argues that the intellectual potential of blacks is restricted by inherent genetic limitations.[25] According to Jensen, it is an improper use of funds to try to improve the status of blacks and the poor. That is, little can be done to correct inequities between blacks and whites because the two groups differ in inherited intelligence.

Others, including Richard Herrnstein, express similar views.[26] And it should be noted that these men preach their ideas to students in two of the better-known universities in the country, the University of California and the University of Chicago, respectively.

THE PRESENT WORK

There appears to be, on the part of some social scientists, a curious need to convey the impression that American society is a progressive one on matters of human rights for black people. Distorted statistics and erroneous data are often used to support this myth. Yet there is overwhelming evidence to the contrary; indeed, there seems to be an eroding of commitment to racial equality, and a general shift to the right on matters pertaining to race and poverty.[27]

A careful analysis of the present status of Afro-Americans reveals that since the citizenship gains of the civil rights movement, there is now an attempt to exaggerate these advances, and in some cases to reverse them. There is an urgent need to demonstrate empirically that many of the assumptions about black people in the United States at the present time are myths, and that the unfortunate victims of American racism are being blamed for the oppression they suffer from an all too often cruel social system.

It is ironic (or is it?) that the very social scientists who claim extraordinary progress on the part of black people are likely to take the position that affirmative action programs in colleges and universities have failed because they were abused by black students. They also claim that the busing of students to achieve racial integration in compliance with court orders has lowered educational performance for white students and exacerbated racial tensions. And on the college level it is their position that open admissions programs have tended to lower educational standards.

Many of the claims made by social scientists are contradictory, and they cannot have it both ways. It is the contention of this work that given the nature of black–white relations in the United States historically and at the present time, these social scientists are engaged in an exercise that attempts to sanctify a myth, namely, that black Americans suffer little, if any, discrimination. They write about race relations in the United States from the naive point of view that in a decade centuries of oppression have been reversed. Social change, especially in the realm of race relations, comes slowly in the United States. At the present rate of change, it is unlikely that parity between blacks and whites will be achieved in the next century because a significant change in race relations calls for a rather fundamental alteration of the institutions of a society in which significant change takes place slowly.

Black social scientists, as well as white, appear to be supporting the growing conservative movement in the United States. That white social scientists should engage in these activities is not surprising. However, black sociologists who support the conservative movement are not unlike government officials in (formerly) South Vietnam who supported American aggression against their own people.

II

ECONOMIC DECLINE AND THE RISE OF THE NEW CONSERVATISM: TWIN THREATS TO BLACKS

WALTER STAFFORD

A N enduring characteristic of black Americans has been their ability to continually adjust to cyclical economic and political setbacks. This ability was severely put to the test in the 1970s. In that decade, their goal of gaining political, economic, and social equality began to seem like a surrealistic dream for many blacks, and a mood of alienation and despair became pervasive in many segments of the black community. In an attempt to understand some of the causes of that despair, this chapter examines the principal economic, social, and political trends of the 1970s and early 1980s that led to new priorities, a rise in conservative ideas,[1] and a reevaluation by blacks of their economic mobility and political participation.

Three distinctive features of the United States in the 1970s and early 1980s were a faltering economy, a growing loss of public confidence in national institutions and leadership, and a heightened debate about political, social, and personal rights, entitlements, values, and moral issues. These three issues, which affected whites and blacks, fused to set the stage for the breakdown of traditional coalitions, the establishment of new alliances, and the emergence of powerful and competing single-issue groups ranging from those concerned with gun control to abortion.[2] (In fact, it has been estimated that in the 1980s as many as 20 million persons were members of or financial contributors to special interest groups.)

Although the issues and the competition resembled the 1960s in some respects, for blacks there was one significant difference. Unlike the debate and unrest of the 1960s, when the concerns of blacks were often at the center of the political and social discourse, the interests of blacks were virtually ignored during the 1970s. The changing nature of the issues

18

that were energizing white social activists, combined with the rise of conservative groups, raised serious problems for blacks. With their economic status deteriorating, and with conservative groups and the Reagan administration posing threats to statutory and constitutional rights won during the last twenty years, blacks often felt threatened and perplexed. These anxieties were exacerbated by the decline of the influence and resources of black organizations and changes in leadership. By the 1970s, the National Urban League, a beneficiary of the greatest federal and private support, was the only broad-based organization with a structure capable of addressing the social and economic problems of blacks, and its resources drastically diminished with the election of Ronald Reagan. The Student Nonviolent Coordinating Committee (SNCC) was defunct, the Southern Christian Leadership Conference (SCLC) was undergoing serious reorganizational problems, the Congress of Racial Equality (CORE) was confronted with internal strife, and the National Association for the Advancement of Colored People (NAACP), which was in serious debt, also had lost a large part of its membership. Moreover, some members of the NAACP's board of directors and the executive director were in open debate about internal policies.

In addition to the change in the resources of organizations, black leadership had undergone rapid changes since the end of the 1960s. Martin Luther King, the leader of the SCLC, had been assassinated; James Farmer, the head of CORE, left the organization in 1966, worked in the Nixon administration, and retired with the American Public Employees; H. Rap Brown of SNCC had been charged with murder in 1970 and spent five years in prison after his surrender; Stokely Carmichael of SNCC was lecturing; Whitney Young, the head of the National Urban League, drowned off the coast of Nigeria in 1971; Vernon Jordan, his successor, resigned in 1982; and Roy Wilkins, head of the NAACP, resigned in 1977. This list is not comprehensive, but it provides an idea of the shift in leadership in less than twenty years.

This breakdown in the phalanx of black leadership and organizational resources resulted in a stalemate in dialogue among blacks about the rapid changes in the political econo-

19

my and limited the number and range of alternatives being
presented to the black community or to white institutions.
Blacks also found themselves with fewer active allies. Several factors combined to create this situation. First, during the
1960s, the "black power" mood, which had been intended to
heighten black consciousness and strengthen black political
cohesiveness, became threatening to many white allies who
became confused about their role in the civil rights struggle.
Second, blacks were increasingly demanding a greater share
of the economic resources as well as political representation.
The quest for economic development of communities, the
establishment of community development corporations, and
control of traditional institutions such as schools meant that
their aims came into conflict with many white supporters.
Third, there was a greater professionalization of traditional
civil rights organizations by blacks, thereby altering the staff
structures in which whites had previously held the professional positions. Fourth, many of the single-issue groups of
the 1970s attracted whites who previously had seen race and
poverty as the most serious issues of the society. Fifth, as
controversy about rights and entitlements increased, notably
those related to affirmative action and meritocracy, blacks
found themselves in open conflict with many of their former
allies. Sixth, as blacks expressed more interest in Third World
politics and the inequities of resource usage by the United
States, they were increasingly viewed with suspicion by those
whites who held liberal views on domestic race relations but
conservative outlooks on the nation's role in the international
economy. The tension had started in the 1960s, when SNCC
expressed support of Third World nations, and reached its
peak in 1979, when United Nations ambassador Andrew
Young attempted to meet with the Palestine Liberation Organization. His attempt was seen as a breach of the U.S. alliance
with Israel, and the incident led to his resignation. The debate
around the issue revealed the differences between blacks and
whites about the role and stance that blacks were expected to
assume on issues of international concern and the support
they could anticipate once they moved away from traditional
questions of racial equality.
    These rapid changes in civil rights organizations and the

which created

20

Economic decline and the new conservatism

deterioration of black–white alliances were occurring during a period of steady decline in the nation's economy. During the 1970s, inflation averaged a little over 7 percent annually, more than triple the average for the previous two decades.[3] Between January 1970 and late October 1979, prices exactly doubled. Unemployment also increased. In 1970 the unemployment rate was 4.9 percent and by 1979 5.3 percent. These changes altered what the public saw as the most critical problems. In 1974, 79 percent of the public listed inflation as the most urgent problem facing the country. By 1982, unemployment, which stood at 9.7 percent, had replaced inflation as the nation's number one problem.[4]

Most groups had to adjust to new economic activities because of new adjustments for the nation in the international economy. This adjustment was only slowly accepted by the public. The first economic jolt for the nation was the oil crisis in 1973–4, when U.S. oil companies found that they could no longer dictate prices to OPEC members. At the time, a large proportion of the public did not believe that a crisis existed,[5] suspecting instead that it was a ploy by oil companies to raise prices. However, as the economy continued to face problems during the decade, the second oil crisis in 1979 was viewed as part of a continuing crisis. By then, other indications of the worsening economic picture were clear, including "stagflation" (simultaneous inflation and unemployment); the closing of plants in the country's heartland; increasing problems of structural unemployment, notably the inability of workers to find jobs even if they moved from economically declining areas to cities where the number of jobs was increasing; and the recognition that most of the standardized products manufactured here could be produced at a higher quality, more cheaply, and more efficiently in other countries.

The economic interests of the United States were challenged on all fronts as developing nations demanded new arrangements for the sharing of resources and challenged the United States' preeminence as the world leader in manufacturing. As U.S. productivity declined, and real wages of workers failed to increase, there was a frantic search for solutions. These included a massive attempt to understand and adopt Japanese management techniques, demands for accelerated

21

education and training, and calls for increased protectionism. By the early 1980s, the nation had developed a quasi–cold war mentality that echoed the 1950s.

The enormity and complexity of the changes, and the almost total absence of answers for pressing questions, left the American public, long accustomed to expanding economic opportunities, confused and anxious. As several analysts observed about the decade, economic security for many middle-class Americans was the precondition for social relations, especially the more recent emphasis on self-fulfillment as a private search outside of traditional institutions.[6] Thus, as the economy declined a growing malaise set in among the public and disillusionment with the inability of political leaders to provide new economic ideas and solutions increased. National leaders were aware of the public's disposition, but few of them had any immediate solutions. This mood of frustration was one of the key reasons for the defeat of Jimmy Carter in 1980, as neither he nor the intellectuals, civil rights activists, union leaders, and business executives who were the backbone of his 1976 winning coalition had answers that could address the malaise.[7]

For Carter and most national leaders, the crises of the 1970s established a new political concern, one in which economic decline rather than unlimited expansion established the framework. In this atmosphere, some analysts, most notably those who wrote the Tri-Lateral Commission's *The Crisis of Democracy*,[8] questioned whether the more liberal and individualized values that had emerged from the economic expansion of prior decades would be adaptable to recessions and resource shortages. And if they did survive, the analysts fretted that they "posed an additional problem for democratic government in terms of its ability to mobilize its citizens for the achievement of social and political goals and to impose discipline and sacrifice on its citizens in order to achieve these goals."[9]

For blacks, the crises of the 1970s meant that new alternatives had to be developed in order to maintain the gains won largely during a period of economic expansion and that new strategies had to be devised in order to obtain their share of limited resources.

The politics of distribution

The concept of restraint in the political arena

Even before the 1980 election, the contours of the problems
facing blacks in the political economy were becoming clear.
The central features of the landscape were constructed
around concepts and debates about "social triage," the "limits
to growth," "zero-sum games," and "political restraint" –
issues that had gained prominence in the late 1960s and early
1970s. Few political leaders were unaware of the debates, and
certainly not Jimmy Carter, who had been a member of the
Tri-Lateral Commission. In his inaugural address in 1976, he
talked about the limits of growth in a refrain that echoed the
themes of *The Crisis of Democracy*[10] and of other analysts
who wrote about the rapid decline of resources during the
period. According to President Carter:

> We have learned that *more* is not necessarily *better*, that even
> our great nation has its recognized limits, and that we can
> neither answer all questions nor solve all problems. We cannot
> afford to do everything, nor can we afford to lack boldness as we
> meet the future. So, together, in a spirit of individual sacrifice
> for the common good, we must simply do our best.[11]

Carter's imprimatur on establishing new arrangements
within an era of economic limitations became a recurring
theme, which he repeated in his New Foundations speech to
the nation in 1979, calling for more restraint at home and a
recognition of a changing international order. The call for
restraint was reinforced by his advisers. In 1979, Stuart
Eizenstat, Carter's chief domestic adviser, defended the par-
ing of social programs by noting that although Carter's commitments to social justice were "as strong – and his accom-
plishments as meaningful as any past Democratic President
. . . every president must face the reality he inherits . . . If the
1960s seemed a time of unlimited expansion, the 1970s seem
to be a time of needed restraint and consolidation – a time to
make the programs of the 1960s work."[12]

To Carter's credit, at least for blacks, he was not asking for
restraint by blacks, although he was reducing many of the

social programs that affected them. The problem for blacks was not necessarily with Carter and his administration, but with the fact that almost all of the groups who had supported or opposed Carter were increasingly involved with new approaches and ideas for structuring the political and social system. Blacks remained Carter's strongest supporters, even with the criticism of him by black leaders for reducing program gains of the 1960s. He appointed record numbers of blacks to middle-level federal positions and judgeships. Moreover, although there were questions about the efforts of his administration in affirmative action, his appointees to the Equal Employment Opportunity Commission and the Office of Federal Contract Compliance Programs ensured black gains. Indeed, at the same time Carter's administration was acting to reduce some of the social programs, the symbiosis between his administration and blacks was clear from his speech at Cheney State, a predominantly black college in Pennsylvania, in which he criticized blacks for not becoming more politically active through voting.[13] However, the narrow debate between Carter and black leaders obscured other changes.

Resource distribution in an era of decline

Although blacks were slow to enter the debate about the distribution of resources in an era of restraint, it had become a major political issue among whites. In New York City, the fiscal crisis in 1975 had sparked a debate about "planned shrinkage" as a way of reducing services to some communities (mainly low income and black) and of prodding low-income groups to leave. The success of Proposition 13 in California reflected the desire of the middle class to reduce property taxes. By 1979, 30 states had voted for a constitutional convention to balance the budget, and a Gallup Survey in 1979 revealed that 78 percent of the public favored a proposed constitutional amendment that would require Congress to balance the federal budget each year.[14]

Politicians of all stripes joined the debate about reductions and curtailment of government spending and taxes during the 1970s. Carter, in his 1976 campaign, had criticized the tax system as so unjust that it was a "disgrace to the human race."[15] And Jerry Brown, one of the most liberal Democrats in the presidential primaries in 1980, was a proponent of a constitutional amendment requiring a federally balanced budget.[16]

These examples reflect the ethos of the period and the efforts of groups to grapple with how resources would be distributed in a declining economy. The problem facing all groups was that few were ready to practice restraint and the political system had no equitable way of assigning losses.

The problem of distribution during a period of economic decline has been addressed by Lester Thurow, who characterized the process as "zero-sum" games, that is, those in which the losses equal the winnings. When there are large losses to be allocated, any economic decision will have a zero-sum result. As Thurow notes, the essence of economic problem solving is loss allocation. Yet this is precisely what the American political process is least capable of doing. Thurow observes: "When there are economic gains to be allocated, our political process can allocate them. When there are large economic losses to be allocated, our political process is paralyzed. And with political paralysis comes economic paralysis."[17]

When the period is characterized as one of zero-sum games, it must be remembered that the late 1960s and 1970s was the first time that blacks had actively demanded economic rewards. Prior to that period they had relied primarily on protest politics to get the courts to ensure their legal and constitutional rights. During the 1960s, when they became a key part of the political process, through protest, they were able to raise the costs for groups who were reluctant or unwilling to consider their demands. However, in the 1970s, in a period of economic decline and with less organizational strength, their demands for an equitable share of resources were often overlooked. National and local political and economic leaders, faced with demands from whites for restraints in spending, were less able to appease the demands of blacks for more resources.

For blacks, the execution of almost all of their programs required substantial expenditures, from the proposals of the late Whitney Young for a domestic Marshall Plan, to proposals by James Foreman, a leader of SNCC, for reparations. Not only would programs for blacks cost money, but blacks were not in positions within government to protect the gains they had won. For example, blacks had just begun to move into leadership positions in local governments where they could protect their interests, and even then they still were not in positions where they controlled agencies with substantial tax levy powers. Consequently, when decisions were made at the local level about the distribution of jobs and resources during the period of restraint, blacks were unable to protect themselves.[18]

What blacks were confronted with in the 1970s was a major shift in the political thinking about distribution of resources. Prior to the 1970s, one way liberalism had muted racial protests was to convert demands for participation and distribution into limited economic gains. The political and economic elites were able to satisfy blacks merely by increasing the total economic pie, so that while not taking anything from those with resources, they were able to increase the rewards for those with few resources. Typically, those at the lower end of the economic scale were satisfied with receiving resources that were relatively uncostly for the elites to yield and they did not challenge established political arrangements, for example, incrementally increased welfare benefits, unemployment compensation, income transfer programs, and Community Action Programs.[19] As a result, blacks and other marginal groups stopped short of demanding major redistribution of resources and political power. The success of this strategy was aided by a materialistic orientation shared by most Americans and an almost universal belief in the evolutionary development of a middle class based on the work ethic and an expanding economy.

With the economic downturn of the 1970s, economic rewards were no longer possible as a soporific for marginal groups. In addition, many middle-class white groups had positioned themselves in the economy so that restraints would not mean large losses. And those with resources definitely were not willing to relinquish them to appease groups at the bottom of the economic ladder. Indeed, one of the effects of the affluent society is that Americans are unwilling to relinquish access to resources in a shrinking economy. Instead, they became more concerned about competitively positioning themselves for access to college and other social and political indexes of status and influence. With a shrinking economic pie, therefore, social, political, and economic rights were vigorously protected.[20]

One major indication of the trend toward positioning was the shift in the definition of the label "minority," which gradually expanded to include women, homosexuals, children, older persons, and various European and Asian ethnic groups. Whereas "rights" were previously pursued almost exclusively by blacks, dozens of groups now began to recognize that they, too, were being deprived of what was "rightfully" theirs.

These debates and ideas sharpened during the decade, and by 1980 and the election of Ronald Reagan, the relationship between race, rights, and resources was clearly articulated by his appointees. In a commencement address at Amherst College in the summer of 1983, Bradford Reynolds, head of the Justice Department's Civil Rights Division, noted:

> *The use of race in the distribution of limited resources in the past decade has regrettably led to the creation of a kind of racial spoils system in America,* fostering competition not only among individual members of contending groups but among the groups themselves. Racial classifications are wrong – morally wrong – and ought not to be tolerated in any form . . . It must be remembered that we are – each of us – a minority of one. Our rights derive from the uniquely American belief in the primacy of the individual. And in no instance should an individual's rights rise any higher or fall any lower than the rights of others because of race.[21]

Although Reynolds's argument is complex, his message is clear.[22] By combining an appeal to American individualism and morality, an attack on political corruption and racism, and a further expansion of the concept of "minority," Reynolds was announcing that special treatment for blacks would no longer be a consideration in the allocation of resources.

What blacks were finding in their efforts to enter the debate about the allocation of resources was that many of the older approaches were no longer viable. At each turn another barrier would be constructed if race was used as a basis for distribution. However, in addition to the issue related to distribution, blacks also faced problems of merely entering the debates.

As economic decline proceeded, the range of issues about rights, morals, and limits of resources increased. And as the issues increased, it became more difficult for blacks to relate race to the competing interests of other groups. Most of the issues of the period – women's rights, abortion, teenage pregnancy, homosexuality, children's rights, the rights of the elderly, nuclear disarmament, etc. – affected blacks. However, to extract and develop a racial component within each of the issues required resources that none of the black organizations had. Moreover, by 1980, the nation's population had become increasingly educated, with 40 percent of the labor force having completed one or more years of college, 22 percent having completed four years of college, and 52 percent working in white-collar occupations. Consequently, many of the issues being dealt with by white groups were often those psychological, social, and moral concerns related to postindustrial capitalism and the greater individualized opportunities and freedoms that had emerged during the 1960s.

While blacks continued to struggle with the problems of race, the debates among whites were increasingly related to other questions regarding the use of resources. The conflict among whites resulted largely from the fact that almost all of the problems of the past, for example, race, class conflict, economic crisis, and distribution of wealth, were still unresolved. As society destigmatized homosexuality, the mystique of women, alcoholism, and a variety of other social and moral problems that had remained hidden before, the question of lifestyle and access to available resources became a sensitive political issue. For example, it was no longer merely a matter of who would get jobs, but also of when people should retire and the level of benefits they should receive.

Blacks were involved in many of these debates. However,

The politics of distribution

most of the postindustrial issues became increasingly difficult to relate to race without further dividing blacks. For example, the issue of sexism and women's rights was rarely dealt with as extensively in the black community as among whites. For black males and females the problem of analyzing the combined effects of racism and sexism became almost impossible.[23]

Another reason whites were able to lower race as an issue was because blacks never threatened their economic security to any great extent during the 1970s. The rules and procedures of most organizations operated to effectively minimize the inclusion and power of blacks. These procedures could be altered to expand or contract opportunities based on the objectives of the organization. Moreover, in the public sector, where blacks made most of their gains during the 1980s, whites were protected by seniority laws, which were altered only through extensive litigation. Blacks and whites in the public sector were not in intense competition, since the agencies in which blacks were usually concentrated in higher-paying jobs were those dealing with social welfare and whites remained in control of agencies dealing with financial matters and intergovernmental relations. The competition in the private sector was usually less intense. Blacks were able to make strong competitive gains in private employment sectors where affirmative action programs were well enforced as a result of consent decrees, such as that between the government and American Telephone and Telegraph.[24] However, even where consent decrees were in existence, the gains of blacks were minimal.[25] Thus, in the private sector of the economy, blacks remained all but excluded from industries such as securities, television, publishing, advertising, and other sectors involved in finance or setting trends in culture and style.

As a result of the changes in issues during the 1970s, views about resource distribution became less skewed toward a concern about groups who had been excluded and more toward finding ways to lessen the problems of downward mobility for those who had benefited from economic gains. The issue for many groups was to find solutions to position themselves against further losses. And these solutions, which be-

29

came increasingly moral and ideological in character, dealt more directly with the leadership and values of institutions.

THE DEBATE ABOUT MORALS AND VALUES ENTERS THE POLITICAL ARENA

If the 1960s represented a time of challenge to institutional authority, a demand for new rights, and a search for new avenues for personal growth, the 1970s represented a time of debate about how these trends affected major institutions in an era of restraint. Many of the movements of the 1960s continued into the 1970s, especially the search for individual self-fulfillment. However, economic decline meant that individualized approaches to politics and social change had to fit into the special group interests and that flexible lifestyles had to be adjusted to lower economic expectations.

As the 1970s unfolded, almost every alternative about rights, culture, and religion became a matter of intense debate. Liberals such as Christopher Lasch questioned the narcissism of the decade, which was seen as an unwillingness of the white educated elite to examine the future in terms of the past; Robert Lekachman questioned whether the new-consciousness message of writers such as Charles Reich could lead anywhere in the new economic realities of the 1970s; and Daniel Yankelovich pointed out the failure of persons in the self-realization movement to examine racism and poverty.[26] Conservatives were also concerned about these trends, especially their effect on the family, church, and schools and the extent to which the "New Class" of managers and professionals in the governmental sectors who maintained these values were adversaries of the business leaders who spawned industrial capitalism. For both liberals and conservatives alike reacted to the lack of political participation, but in different ways. Liberals lamented the lost opportunity to alter the structure in the political economy or maintain programs that benefited workers, whereas conservatives seized the opportunity to promote alternatives to the liberal programs of prior decades.

Blacks were excluded from significant discussions of both

groups. The debates were among whites and about how they saw their future. Blacks were often perceived as the bête noire as a result of stimulating the rights explosion, as well as the mistaken perception by both liberals and conservatives that many of the permissive trends in sex and drugs had originated in black lifestyles. Conservatives and right-wing groups were aided by three interrelated trends. The first was the emergence of Political Action Committees (PACS),which permitted groups on the right to raise large sums of money from small donors that they in turn used to defeat politicians with liberal views. The second was the greater emphasis by the public on religion, especially fundamental evangelicalism, which absorbed many of the frustrations about the economy and projected white evangelical ministers and mainline church leaders into the political arena. The third was the greater recognition of the ideas of conservative intellectuals.

Political Action Committees had become prominent after the enactment of federal election reforms emanating from the Watergate crisis. With changes in the federal election laws, the amount that individuals could contribute to a specific candidate was limited and groups therefore began to concentrate on smaller donors. There were various types of PACs, which were generally divided into corporate; trade, membership, and health; labor; and ideological. Their emergence and significance can be gleaned by the fact that while there were only 516 registered PACs in 1974,[27] there were 3,479 by the 1981–2 election cycles.[28] It is estimated that during the early 1970s, PACs were growing at a rate of one per day.[29] Conservative ideological PACs developed well-honed mass mailings to small donors and raised millions of dollars. By the early 1980s, the corporate PACs had also become a major force, thereby providing another powerful conservative interest group.

The second phenomenon, the continued growth of religion, had begun in the 1960s. Americans were a nation of people searching for values and meaning. Although the percentage of persons who belonged to a church or synagogue was not as high as in the past, over 60 percent indicated that they belonged to a church or synagogue,[30] and 65 percent indicated that religion can answer problems.[31] In none of the advanced market nations with an educational level as high as the United States was participation in religious institutions as great.

In the 1980 election there were two born-again Christians running, Carter and Anderson, and Ronald Reagan went to extreme efforts to prove his religious faith and to court evangelical voters. Of all the religious activities in the 1970s, it was perhaps the incursions of white fundamentalist ministers into politics and their links with organizers of the ideological PACs that was a major turning point in the debates about many of the previously discussed issues. They not only fed on the frustrations of groups about political and economic changes but also on their personal concerns about abortion, school prayer, and other issues. *U.S. News and World Report* characterized the evangelical ministers' thrust into politics as a "sleeping giant."[32]

The New Right

The conservative groups of the 1970s can be described under three labels: the New Right, which was the political arm, the religious Right, and the neoconservatives, which provided the intellectual foundation. In the forefront was the New Right, a term coined by Kevin Phillips, an author, a former Nixon aide, and one of the key designers of the New Right's political strategy.[33] The New Right was led mainly by young white males, and although most had considerable political experience, they were not, in the main, elected politicians. They emerged during the late 1960s at a time when the political Right was disorganized and unable to effectively articulate challenges to the political, social, and economic positions of the mainstream of the two major parties. Although the John Birch Society and followers of George Wallace had desperately tried to capture and project the mood of the public, none was as effective as the New Right in the 1970s.

The New Right emerged in 1974 as a response to Gerald Ford's nomination of Nelson Rockefeller for the vice-presidency on the Republican ticket. At that time, Richard Viguerie, who was to become the leading fund raiser for the New Right, was incensed by the Republicans' endorsement of what he viewed as the party's liberal Eastern establishment.[34] Calling together other disaffected conservatives, he formed the coalition that was to become known as the New Right. As the movement developed, its network of allies eventually included the American Conservative Union headed by Phyllis Schlafly, which claimed 300,000 members; Young Americans for Freedom; public-interest law firms; law-and-order groups such as the National Rifle Association; profamily groups; and anti-Equal Rights Amendment (ERA) groups. According to Viguerie, the New Right borrowed from liberals its focus on "single-issue politics," uniting opponents of abortion, ERA, and sexual permissiveness.[35]

The activities of the New Right were financed through funds from foundations such as the Heritage and Robert M. Schuchman foundations; businessmen such as Joseph Coors, the brewer of Coors beer; and powerful PACs, including the National Conservative Political Action Committee, which was the leading PAC in gross receipts in 1979; the National Congressional Club, a spinoff of the network of organizations of Senator Jesse Helms (R-NC); Citizens for the Republic; and Committee for the Survival of a Free Congress. These PACs were the major arm of the political thrust of the New Right and among the leading PACs in terms of gross receipts.

Viguerie observed that the New Right was "spurred into taking a technological lead in fundraising because the right had lost so many political battles and because its causes got poor exposure on television and in newspapers."[36] Direct mail solicitation allowed the New Right PACs to bypass what Viguerie considered the liberal media and go directly into the homes of conservatives.[37] The impact of the conservative, ideological PACs on the 1980 elections was particularly significant. With vast sums of money and a network of organizations, groups, and individuals, they transformed the national political scene and developed new methods to attack liberal causes and personalities. The conservative issues they promoted became the basis for their campaigns against liberals, and often these campaigns were extremely vicious. For example, their strategy to defeat George McGovern in 1980 began almost two years before the election and included direct mailings, a media blitz, and brochures and flyers with a picture of a dead fetus and George McGovern's face slashed with a large X, along with the statement, "He has continuously voted tax dollars to kill preborn children."[38]

In 1980, the New Right focused on Democrats and Republicans alike, but their principal targets were liberal senators, including Frank Church of Idaho, Burch Bayh of Indiana, John Culver of Iowa, Alan Cranston of California, and Thomas Eagleton of Missouri. Only Cranston and Eagleton survived. The others were replaced by New Right senators, giving the Republicans their first majority in thirty years. It is widely estimated that at least half of the sixteen Republican newcomers elected in 1980 were there because of the efforts of the political and religious far Right.[39]

These newcomers in the Senate were especially concerned with what they perceived as moral and civil rights issues. Along with the conservatives who were already part of the body, they immediately set about introducing legislation or amendments on abortion, busing, school prayer, sex education in schools, and chastity among teenagers. Roger Jepsen of Iowa introduced the "Family Protection Act," which would exclude corporal punishment methods applied by a parent from child abuse laws, deny federal funds to schools that do not allow parental review of textbooks prior to their use in public school classrooms, prevent schools from using federal money to buy educational materials that present an overly progressive view of the status of men and women, and permit schools receiving federal funds to limit or prohibit the intermingling of the sexes in any sport or other school-related activity.[40] In addition to these human rights issues, the Republican senators initiated Congressional hearings on the constitutionality of affirmative action.

The power and influence of the broad coalition of New Right organizations cannot be overestimated. One analyst called it the fourth most powerful political force in the nation.[41] Alan Crawford noted that it fed on "discontent, anger, insecurity and resentment, and flourished on backlash politics."[42] Leaders of this coalition believed that by forging a "new majority" they could ultimately attract the new black middle class that was fearful of crime and related issues.[43] However, their main thrust during the 1970s was to work around issues that would lead to mobilization of whites who were frightened and frustrated by the rapid changes of the 1960s and 1970s. Without question they were one of the main reasons Reagan was elected, and they consistently prodded him in his first three years to remain committed to their causes.

The religious Right

An important ally of the New Right was the religious evangelicals, which included the Moral Majority, the Religious Roundtable, and the National Christian Action Coalition. White ministers who had sat on the sidelines during the civil rights movement of the 1960s became energetically involved in politics during the 1970s, supporting many of the aforementioned issues and decrying what they considered secular morality and the erosion of values in the nation. It has been estimated that evangelical ministers, led by Rex Humbard, Robert Schuller, and Jerry Falwell, reached at least 50 million viewers on their weekly television shows. In 1980, one in eight of the nation's radio stations carried at least fourteen hours of religious programming; 600 of them offered it full time; and religious radio stations were being founded at one per week.[44]

The major group among the evangelicals was the Moral Majority, led by the Reverend Jerry Falwell from headquarters in Lynchburg, Virginia. With the Moral Majority in the vanguard, the religious Right became more politically aggressive, which brought them critics from both the Left and the Right. In 1980, sixty-one prominent scholars and writers issued a declaration attacking the absolutist morality espoused by Christian fundamentalists and warning against the simplistic and emotional solutions they advocated.[45] They were also criticized by conservatives and liberals. Conservatives saw them as a disrupting force,[46] and liberals saw in them a new threat to the ideals of liberal education as well as pluralism, civil rights, and religious and personal freedoms.[47] Despite opposition from all fronts, the Christian Right was a powerful political force in the 1980 election, overtaking some state and local party organizations in the primaries.

They also needled presidential candidates on social and moral issues. Although Anderson and Carter, the most out-

35

spokenly religious candidates, largely rejected their appeal, Reagan blatantly catered to their priorities. During the campaign, he vowed to end the federal government's "unconstitutional regulatory vendetta" against independent religious schools,[48] endorsed prayer in the schools, and challenged the teaching of Darwinian theories of evolution.[49]

The influence of religion in politics was significant in elections in 1976 and 1980. In the 1976 election, Jimmy Carter, a born-again Christian, won 46 percent of the Protestant vote. In the 1980 election, however, the evangelicals abandoned Carter, feeling that he had moved too far to the left, and gave their support to the more conservative candidate, Ronald Reagan. Although some analysts believe that the fundamentalists were given too much credit for Reagan's victory, it is unarguable that they influenced the Republican platform, exerted a powerful influence on Ronald Reagan's campaign, and have continued to affect his political rhetoric. Echoes of his 1980 campaign were heard in his 1983 speech to the National Association of Evangelicals, in which he stated:

> This administration is motivated by a political philosophy that sees the greatness of America in you, her people, and in your families, churches, neighborhoods, communities – the institutions that foster and nourish values like concern for others and respect for the rule of law under God . . . There is sin and evil in the world, and we are enjoined by Scripture and the Lord Jesus to oppose it with all our might. Our nation, too, has a legacy of evil with which it must deal. The glory of this land has been its capacity for transcending the moral evils of our past . . . The real crisis we face today is a spiritual one; at root, it is a test of moral will and faith.[50]

In his speech Reagan tried to separate racism from what he considered the underlying philosophy of religious and political conservatism. Indeed, as shown later, a tenet of his administration was to separate racial, social, and religious issues. However, the interrelationships of his appeal to conservative groups and his efforts to reduce programs for blacks combined to weaken denials of racism in the administration's policies.

The debate about morals and values

The third part of the conservative phalanx during the 1970s was the intellectuals. Although intellectuals such as Kevin Phillips were sprinkled among the New Right, most of the conservative scholars, writers, and academicians of the period were identified as neoconservatives. Like the New Right, the leaders were usually white males. However, unlike their tenuous ally, the neoconservatives were older, better known, and less strident in their crusade for conservative change.

The label was coined by the socialist writer Michael Harrington to describe former liberals who had moved to the right and embraced conservative ideas. The men and women generally identified under the banner included many of the nation's better-known intellectuals. Peter Steinfels, whose book the *Neo-Conservatives* is the most extensive analysis of the personalities and ideas of the leading males in the group, notes that "it will not do justice to the special position of the Neo-Conservatives to describe them simply as a party of intellectuals, as though that fact alone justified their claim to our attention. The Neo-Conservatives are a *powerful* party of intellectuals."[51]

Although many intellectuals who were so labeled disowned the neoconservative brand, a partial list of those identified under the banner includes Daniel Bell, a sociologist; Robert Nisbet, sociologist; James Q. Wilson, political scientist; Norman Podhoretz, the editor of *Commentary;* Irving Kristol, a leading social critic and an editor of *Public Interest;* Daniel Moynihan, United States senator and social and political analyst; Michael Novak, social scientist; Nathan Glazer, sociologist; Samuel Huntington, the political scientist discussed earlier in reference to the Tri-Lateral Commission; Sidney Hook, philosopher; Midge Decter, writer; Ben Wattenburg, author and analyst; Jeanne Kirkpatrick, political scientist and United States ambassador to the United Nations; and dozens more well-known and impeccably credentialed white men and women.

Intellectual conservatism was not new in America. However, it had never been organized into a coherent body of thought. Traditional conservatives usually considered themselves disciples of Edmund Burke, the eighteenth-century English philosopher, and had widely extolled the role of tradition, authority, and the need to be circumspect about social change, but it was the neoconservatives of the late 1960s and 1970s who provided conservatism its broadest acceptance. The ideas promoted by the neoconservatives were often incorporated in high-level debates on political and economic issues. Moreover, because of their credentials and expertise, many of the neoconservatives were appointed to key governmental positions or served as consultants to several presidents (from Kennedy to Reagan). They were ensconced in the most elite universities and were among the leaders arguing against integration of faculties. In addition, neoconservatives were editors of two of the leading intellectual and policy journals in the 1970s, *Commentary* and *Public Interest*. These magazines provided them with a forum for promoting and debating critical ideas. Both magazines were widely read among intellectuals, and *Public Interest* was a major organ for discussion of policies on almost every social, economic, and political problem in the nation.

The neoconservatives were also part of an expanding network of respected research organizations. They had associations with the Hoover Institution at Stanford and were considered a major link to the American Enterprise Institute and the Center for Strategic and Internal Studies of Georgetown University.

The ideas of the neoconservatives were broad in scope. Although they disagreed about issues related to homosexuality and women's rights, they were drawn together by their anticommunism, opposition to busing, and many aspects of affirmative action (especially what they considered intrusion into higher education). They were also disillusioned by the social experimentation of the 1960s and the poverty programs of the Great Society era. Although Moynihan in particular had been involved in the ideas that led to the programs, he had become concerned that the government did not know what it was doing when it tried to implement the theories of social scientists that had led to the poverty programs.[52] He maintained that the programs promised more than they could deliver and that with the upsurge of politicization of the programs by blacks they became a political liability to federal officials. Although conceding that not enough research or evaluation had been conducted on the programs, he questioned from the basis of the poor's involvement in decision making in these programs whether they would ever be ready to assume power in an advanced society.[53] Moynihan's views generally reflected those of other neoconservatives. The neoconservatives, in the main, reacted to the rapid changes of the 1960s. Several additional factors united them. One was their reaction to the New Left and what they saw as the limits of liberalism. Although the New Left became a source of disdain for many older white radicals, such as Irving Howe,[54] they were viewed with particular suspicion by the neoconservatives.

Neoconservatives, notably Huntington and Moynihan, were also concerned with the excessive demands being made on society's institutions. They were concerned that because of the growing public expectations of institutions that leaders of institutions could not meet, there would be a loss of confidence in leadership and institutions.

These ideas about authority, liberalism, and demands also were reflected in the writings of Irving Kristol, who was especially concerned about the growth of the "new class." Kristol noted that mass higher education in the United States had spawned a new elitist group under the banner of the "new politics." He further claimed that this group had driven President Johnson from office and nominated McGovern for president in 1972. He numbered the new class in the millions and said that it included scientists, lawyers, educators, city planners, social workers, and doctors and that the majority worked in the public sector. In Kristol's view:

> They are acting upon a hidden agenda: to propel the nation from that modified version of capitalism we call the "welfare state" toward an economic system so stringently regulated in detail as to fulfill many of the traditional anti-capitalist aspirations of the Left . . . The exact nature of what has been happening is obscured by the fact that this "new class" is not merely liberal but truly "libertarian" in its approach to all areas of life except economics.[55]

39

Economic decline and the new conservatism

In Kristol's estimation, the reason the new class had met such little resistance was that they were a constant source of energy within the capitalist system. He stated that capitalism breeds its own discontents, but if left alone without strong antagonisms it can cope with much of the resulting conflict, which is at root a class conflict, through economic growth and aspects of the welfare state. However, the new class believed that the manner in which the market satisfied the ordinary person was distasteful, and they were trying to supersede the economy through politics, at which they were highly competent. Kristol's solution was for corporations to use their resources to educate those in the new class who were not wedded to its philosophy and to use their funds and the resources of foundations to give support to those who shared their belief in the autonomy of the private sector. He concluded that it would be fruitless to talk about saving "free enterprise." However, in Kristol's view the corporate sector had a major stake in protecting its interests against the new class in the war of ideas.[56]

Other concerns dealt with equality. Neoconservatives saw the drive for equality as a major social force in the nation and as being propelled by liberal intellectuals. In the view of neoconservatives, the idea of equality had taken on dangerous significance because it was not the lower classes but the new class and liberals who were promoting change in almost every aspect of life. Kristol in particular saw the class struggle between the business sector and the liberal intellectuals as being conducted under the banner of "equality." According to Kristol:

> We have an intelligentsia which so despises the ethos of bourgeois society, and which is so guilt ridden at being implicated in the life of this society, that it is inclined to find even collective suicide preferable to the status quo . . . We have a "new class" of self-designated "intellectuals" who share much of this attitude but who, rather than committing suicide, pursue power in the name of equality . . . *And then we have the ordinary people, working-class and lower-middle-class, basically loyal to the bourgeois order but confused and apprehensive at the lack of clear meaning in this order – a lack derived from the increasing bureaucratization (and accompanying impersonalization) of*

political and economic life. All of these discontents tend to express themselves in terms of "equality" which is in itself a quintessentially bourgeois ideal and slogan.[57]

The neoconservatives were also concerned about the manner in which the concept of equality was being expanded in terms of affirmative action programs. Irving Howe has noted that part of the neoconservative impulse is based on the "tremendous difficulties" of achieving racial integration and that many whites who gained from the welfare state programs in the 1930s and 1940s felt threatened by measures designed to remedy "the unmeasured handicaps of millions of blacks."[58]

These were strong negative reactions by the neoconservatives to affirmative action, especially as they construed the difference between providing *equality of opportunity* and *equality of conditions.* Equality of opportunity was not generally opposed by neoconservatives. However, governmental efforts to impose equality of conditions for minorities and women or to establish quotas were firmly rejected. Under equality of opportunity employers would be told that discrimination was wrong and that qualified *individuals* should be sought out. By contrast, under equality of conditions specific *groups* would be identified based on need. To neoconservatives, equality of conditions rejected the principles of meritocracy – which most neoconservatives supported – in favor of compensation for past discriminatory practices. Their arguments have been presented best in Nathan Glazer's book, *Affirmative Discrimination: Ethnic Inequality and Public Policy.*[59] Glazer's arguments against affirmative action programs are as follows:

1 Blacks made most of their gains in employment during the 1960s, before the adoption of affirmative action policies by the federal government requiring statistical comparisons and adjustments to underutilization. In effect, since blacks made employment gains without strong governmental intervention, it was enough to have programs that promoted equal opportunity.
2 Affirmative action efforts had spawned a bureaucracy that was another intrusion into business and higher educational decision making.

41

3 Affirmative action programs were not reaching the black poor.
4 The creation of fixed ethnic-racial categories for preferential hiring would spread.
5 New racial and ethnic antagonism would be created among groups.
6 Compensation for the past is a dangerous principle. As echoed by Bradford Reynolds's speech in 1983, Glazer notes: "We are indeed a nation of minorities; to enshrine some minorities as deserving of special benefits means not to defend minority rights against a discriminatory majority but to favor some of these minorities over others."[60]

The ideas of the neoconservatives were expansive. However, in most cases, but especially in regard to race and affirmative action, they overstated the dangers. For example, the number of federal employees in agencies enforcing affirmative action was small; most of the gains by blacks in the 1960s were in the public sector and not in universities or the private sector; and most employers were able to set broad affirmative action goals that federal agencies, because of their small staffs, could not monitor or check. Irrespective of their tendency to overstate the dangers of the pursuit of equality of conditions, the new class, and the threats to authority, they were widely listened to. Their arguments essentially were against any redistribution of wealth and resources outside of the marketplace and a rejection of efforts for assistance to blacks and other minorities based on past discrimination. They also feared that the new class of younger, more liberal professionals would use their political strength to alter existing patterns based on their views of equality. They believed that authority must be reasserted and government protected and that individuals and groups needed to lower their expectations. Peter Steinfels notes that the neoconservatives initially started out with penetrating and useful questions. But he warned that should their ideas become implemented through political action, they could threaten, attenuate, and diminish the promise of American democracy.[61]

The impact of each of the three groups – the New Right, the religious right, and the neoconservatives – on the politics and ideas of the 1970s cannot be overstated. Although the groups disagreed on many points, the ideas they espoused were exceedingly dangerous to blacks and to the liberal ideas developed over the decades. Seven aspects of their shared perspectives and values stand out as particularly important for blacks:

1 All groups were intent on using the media to promote their ideas. Black issues were often ignored, and blacks did not have the resources to compete against them.

2 Religious symbolism, morals, and values were joined together to strengthen conservative arguments for a return to respect for leadership and authority. For blacks such arguments were dangerous, since most institutional leadership had ingrained into its decision-making processes various aspects of institutional racism. Consequently, the concept of a return to basics with respect to traditional authority was extremely dangerous.

3 The "profamily" emphasis of all conservatives often implied that family instability was the underlying cause rather than the result of economic problems in the black community.

4 Almost all of the conservative groups opposed affirmative action. They also stressed the conflict that could occur between groups, even though surveys revealed the opposite. Finally, their emphasis on individualism and meritocracy ignored the realities of the system. They themselves often showed that a variety of factors influenced one's chances. Their intention was to deemphasize the validity of rewards and resource allocations made on the basis of race and to emphasize the dangers to "individual rights."

5 Most of the groups argued that the market should determine social benefits. Thus, they were adamantly against the social experiments of the 1960s, with the exception of programs such as Head Start and Medicare.

6 Almost all of the groups opposed busing as a means of integrating schools and characterized it as an abrogation of local authority.

7 They addressed their appeals to different classes, but the message was the same. They claimed that, at root, the disaffection within the public was caused by the growth of liberalism, which although spawned by mass education and the beneficence of business could now destroy them. The New Right's appeal was to the middle class, with a special focus on entrepreneurs, whom they encouraged to become

43

less benevolent to those groups that did not necessarily share their views. The Moral Majority addressed the white working classes and the middle class, and the neoconservatives targeted the corporate sector and alienated intellectuals. Their disdain for the New Left and liberalism had important implications for black professional and managerial groups, who were not widely accepted by the groups comprising the so-called new class. If the new class was seen as adversaries, then certainly black groups who did not support corporate aims would be viewed even less favorably.

By the early 1980s there were tensions between the groups. Each claimed it was responsible for Reagan's victory. Moreover, each of them was upset with Reagan for not being conservative enough during his first two years. The New Right thought he did not go far enough to the right on social issues and they were upset about some aspects of his foreign policy. The religious Right thought that his stands were not strong enough on abortion and prayer in the schools. The neoconservatives were troubled by his foreign policy and his failure to consult them frequently enough, even though their ideas were clearly adopted. One of the first strategies of conservative presidents, for example, was to dismantle agencies where a black new class could emerge as potential regulators of and consequently a threat to business and other institutions. Additionally, the New Right and the neoconservatives were well aware that this was their first opportunity since the 1950s to promote their ideas and programs.

For blacks and their allies the fact that the conservative coalition was splintering during the early 1980s brought little consolation, for they did not have strong alternatives to the movement. An indication of the waning influence of conservative groups was that Ronald Reagan was not elected with a conservative mandate. Studies reveal that Reagan's victory was more the result of the pervasive mood that it was "time for a change" rather than a shift to conservatism. Moreover, commercial surveys revealed that voters considered the Reagan administration substantially more conservative than themselves.[62] The fact that blacks were unable to take advantage of this discrepancy deserves special attention.

Although the recent economic decline has had a devastating effect on the black community, black organizations and leaders have been involved only peripherally in discussions about economic development and new directions for the nation's social policy. For the most part, traditional civil rights and social service organizations such as the NAACP and the National Urban League attacked the Reagan administration's policies but did not mount strong challenges to the far-reaching social philosophy of conservative groups or offer substantive ideas about restructuring the economy. Their primary involvement in economic policy and development during the 1960s and early 1970s had been as federally funded trainers of the unemployed and underemployed, strong advocates of increased governmental support for minority businesses, and beneficiaries and administrators of affirmative action programs. When these programs were reduced by the Reagan administration, the link between civil rights organizations and economic decision makers was severed. Since that time, black leadership, including black elected officials, has appeared uncertain about how to effectively confront the new forces of the Right, and their strategies for assisting low-income blacks have been slow to develop.

Blacks, unable to marshal broad ideological or strategic attacks on conservatives, have waged an ineffective battle as the Reagan administration weakened affirmative action programs and reduced funds for social programs that had benefited many blacks. Although there have been attempts to revive the alliances of blacks and liberal whites around issues of poverty and jobs, these coalitions have not regained the strength they displayed in the 1960s. Indeed, in the 1983 March on Washington, in which 250,000 persons massed to demonstrate against federal policies and continued joblessness, the National Urban League declined to participate (citing the march's lack of focus) and other black leaders also questioned its efficacy. Thus, the moderate black leadership is becoming increasingly isolated from many of the broader demands for social, political, and economic change. Available evidence indicates that the nation has not turned conservative. However, the challenges posed by conservatives have until now gone unmet by blacks.

III

CLASS AND RACE IN AMERICA

THE question of whether class or race is the more salient variable in race relations in the United States has plagued scholars since the early part of the twentieth century. Initially class was assumed by the more progressive scholars and organizations to be the crucial factor, for class was considered to be a Marxist concept. In the 1980s, however, class as a concept has been championed by conservative scholars, both black and white. The issue is a complicated one, and does not lend itself to an easy choice, for the two concepts are obviously related. Afro-Americans, for example, are subjected to both racial oppression and economic exploitation, and the task of saying which is the more salient in their daily lives is difficult. Indeed, which is more crucial may be a function of the situation. In some situations race may be the dominant factor; in others it may be class.

According to Karl Marx, societies tend to be divided into two classes, the proletariat (exploited) and the bourgeoisie (exploiters). The latter are the owners of the means of production, whereas the former constitute the working class. In Marx's analysis there is the assumption that there exists a solidarity of the lower classes against the higher ones, and that solidarity between the lower classes will emerge as a matter of natural development.

In *The Communist Manifesto* Marx and Engels make it clear that for them the existence of classes and the class struggle are fundamental components of all noncommunist societies. They write:

> The history of all hitherto existing society is the history of class struggles. Freeman and slave, patrician and plebeian, lord and serf, guild-master and journeyman, in a word oppressor and

oppressed, stood in constant opposition to one another, carried on an uninterrupted, now hidden, now open fight, a fight that each time ended either in a revolutionary reconstitution of society at large, or in the common ruin of the contending classes. In the earlier epochs of history, we find almost everywhere a complicated arrangement of society into various orders, a manifold gradation of social rank . . . The modern bourgeois society that has sprouted from the ruins of feudal society has not done away with class antagonisms. It has but established new classes, new conditions of oppression, new forms of struggle in the place of the old ones. Our epoch, the epoch of the bourgeoisie, possesses, however, this distinctive feature; it has simplified the class antagonisms. Society as a whole is more and more splitting up into two great hostile camps, into two great classes directly facing each other: Bourgeoisie and Proletariat.[1]

Although Marxist scholarship has never been fully accepted in American academic circles, this has changed somewhat in the past decade or two because it is the only theory that explains diverse sets of facts in a consistent manner. Pure Marxism is an ideology that allows one to predict, with some degree of accuracy, the philosophy and views of those who adhere to it.

More than 100 years after the publication of *The Communist Manifesto,* Mao Tse-tung, in a statement supporting Afro-Americans "in their just struggle against racial discrimination by U.S. Imperialism," had this to say: "In the final analysis, national struggle is a matter of class struggle. Among the whites in the United States it is only the reactionary ruling circles who oppose the black people. They can in no way respect the workers, farmers, revolutionary intellectuals and other enlightened persons who comprise the overwhelming majority of white people."[2]

It has been suggested that capitalism is the cause of racism and economic exploitation, and that blacks in the United States are victims of national oppression. The national question has been around for some time, but it gained international attention in 1928 when the Communist Party issued its resolution "On the Negro question in the United States," in which it called for "self-determination of Negroes in the Black Belt" of the South.[3] On the assumption that the proletarian revolution was imminent, in 1935, the Communist Party quickly abandoned its stand on nationalism for one of equal rights for blacks within the United States.

The position that blacks in the United States formed a national minority gained prominence during the civil rights movement, especially in the late 1960s and early 1970s. Those who defined themselves as cultural nationalists (as opposed to revolutionary nationalists) were in the vanguard of this movement.[4] Cultural nationalists rejected Marxist notions of class and class struggle, and Western values, in favor of temporary autonomy for black people and the cultivation of a different value system. Marxists, on the other hand, continued to view the race problem in the United States as largely one of social class.

For example, one historian, in an analysis of Afro-American history from Reconstruction to the first decade of the present century, concludes that

> while racism has been present in American history, it has not been causal. To understand the behavior of the various white groups toward blacks, and blacks toward whites, one must understand the larger forces at work and the structures of power in the society. By reifying and isolating race consciousness and racism, these relationships are ignored, with the result that the function of racism in maintaining the power of the bourgeoisie is distorted, and we are led to believe that men make history according to their racial likes and dislikes.[5]

Such a position is not shared by many black scholars, and although most of them agree that class plays a key role in capitalist America, they see race as the crucial factor in black–white relations, and the evidence they provide is convincing. In the United States blacks tend to be concentrated in the lower socioeconomic groups, and the nature of the society reinforces their subordinate position. Furthermore, although a middle- or upper-status black person might receive a certain amount of deference, in America he or she is ultimately just another black person, one who is seen as somewhat innately inferior.

An eminent black scientist expressed this view as he recounted his experiences for a newspaper: "A second depressing experience recently was to cast off my role as a comfortable, respected scientist and, dressed in work clothes and shoes and an old cap, to walk through the streets to see again just how 'an ordinary Negro' is treated. I shall never forget the abuse, cursing and indignities heaped upon me as I 'accidentally' made a few harmless mistakes . . . I had almost forgotten that I was an angry man."[6]

M. F. Ashley Montagu sees racism as a part of a larger phenomenon of class prejudice. He writes: "The point I wish to bring out here is that 'race' prejudice is merely a special case of class prejudice, a prejudice that will be developed under certain conditions, where different ethnic groups are thrown together in significant numbers. In the absence of such conditions or in the absence of a variety of ethnic groups the prejudices of the upper classes against the lower classes and their conduct toward the members of such classes will, in almost every respect, take the form that is usually associated with 'race' prejudice."[7] Montagu sees class conflict as a broader concept than racism, and racism is but one manifestation of the larger problem. According to his reasoning, wherever classes are present one can find class prejudice. In his analysis the existence of minorities in a society is not a necessary condition for race prejudice.

A recent work on the subject takes the position that race is simply a factor manipulated in the interest of class.[8] Furthermore, the author sees racism as being functional in that it continues to keep blacks oppressed as they were enslaved for centuries. But racism is not sufficiently broad to account for all forms of discrimination; in some cases although it might appear to be crucial, it is possible that race was not at all involved. On the other hand, segregation in the South related to the formation of the ruling class; blacks were the instruments through which whites could resolve their differences. Blacks were convenient scapegoats around which whites could rally and vent their frustrations. The advantage for them was that their white skin automatically conveyed higher status than that of blacks.

Racism is a rationalized ideology that, in the American case, posits blacks and other people of color as innately inferior. History and environment are not related to this alleged inferiority; it is a function of genetics. The presumed inferiority of people of color permits whites to treat them as somewhat less than human. Hence, racism is accompanied by prejudice and discrimination. Sometimes the racism has been so intense that it has led to violence in which blacks are usually slaughtered by whites. If they are perceived as being less than human there is no reason for them to be treated as the equals of white people. Since racists see so-called black inferiority as innate, it follows that these differences are permanent. Intermarriage between the races should not be permitted because the offspring will inherit some of these unfavorable characteristics.

Harold M. Baron has chronicled "the web of urban racism" in the United States, demonstrating that "racism's roots are now firmly embedded in the urban environment."[9] He focuses on racism in housing and land planning, education, and politics, illustrating how in each of these essential areas it is race, not social class, that determines the life chances of Afro-Americans.

While recognizing the importance of class in the United States, Robert Blauner sees race as the more salient of the two variables. The two are related in ways that affect each other. According to Blauner,

> Racism excludes a category of people from participation in a society in a different way than class hegemony and exploitation. The thrust of racism is to dehumanize, to violate dignity and degrade personalities in a much more pervasive and all-inclusive way than class exploitation – which in the United States, at any rate, has typically not been generalized beyond the "point of production." Racist oppression attacks selfhood more directly and thoroughly than does class oppression . . . Class exploitation does not per se stimulate ethnic and national cultures and liberation movements; colonialism and domestic racism do.[10]

It is therefore impossible to reduce race relations to class relations.

Many American scholars maintain that blacks were initially enslaved because of economic, rather than racial, reasons. That is, they see racism as more a product than a cause of slavery.[11] They maintain that racism developed as a result of slavery to justify the enslavement of Afro-Americans. For these scholars, the expansion of modern European capitalism gave rise to modern racism. Does it then follow that if there had been no need for the expansion of capitalism the world would not have experienced racism? It seems unlikely. The phenomenon of racism has so enveloped the globe that if not capital expansion, then something else would have brought it about. Furthermore, with few exceptions, the colonizers focused on countries inhabited by people of color.

Robert Staples concurs with Blauner. He feels that Marx did not adequately deal with the question of racial conflict as a crucial factor in the class struggle. "It is difficult to foresee a unity of Black and white workers when racist attitudes are most strongly ingrained in the working class stratum of American society."[12] Although it must be admitted that racist ideology is likely to be most overt in the working class, it should be remembered that the ideology is also strong among the ruling class, for its members benefit from the arrangement. Nevertheless, those who call for an alliance between white and black workers not only minimize the importance of racism, but as Gunnar Myrdal has pointed out about Reconstruction, "these two groups, illiterate and insecure in an impoverished South, placed in an intensified competition with each other, lacking every trace of primary solidarity, and marked off from each other by color and tradition, could not possibly be expected to clasp hands."[13] Myrdal then cites a Swedish proverb: "when the feed-box is empty, the horses will bite each other."

Historically American white workers have seized on their whiteness as a means of keeping blacks exploited. For them it was their race that elevated them to a position over blacks, not their skills. Although they may have been encouraged by white employers who were mainly interested in keeping all workers oppressed, the white workers were more concerned with race consciousness than class consciousness. Furthermore, while many lynch mobs were organized and abetted by members of the ruling class, lynch mobs were made up largely of members of the working class, who appeared to enjoy their barbaric activities.

Another scholar who views race as more important than

51

class is Joseph Scott. He writes of the early United States: "The first legislative and judicial acts were racist political acts rather than racist economic acts. Curtailment of political social participation preceded curtailment of economic participation. Separation of the races socially and politically preceded separation of the races economically . . . Racism, as such, operates as a free floating force: It can and does enter into decisions without economic content."[14]

One of the difficulties with which black people have been forced to contend is the pervasiveness of racism in the United States. Class prejudice is also widespread, but in most cases racial prejudice is more penetrating. Early on in American history color became the badge of inferiority. Black Americans constitute the only group in the society to be labeled innately inferior. Such a designation has served through the centuries to justify the oppression of black people. Although the white ruling class might have initiated this campaign as a means of assuring a cheap labor supply, it is significant that this designation was reserved for black people and that it has continued.

Earl Ofari sees both race and class as significant obstacles to black progress in the United States, but he appears to give primacy to race, for as he points out, "Blacks are not just discriminated against, they suffer national oppression. The oppressor is not simply the white ruling class but white America, including a large segment of workers who have directly benefited from this national oppression." He concludes that "the biggest single thing which has blunted much of the impact of the class struggle in America has been racism . . . over the decades racism has developed a separate character and taken on new dimensions. Racism so pervades the American psyche that most whites, particularly 'liberals' and 'radicals,' are not even aware of it."[15]

Whatever its origin, as Ofari points out, through the years racism has achieved a functional autonomy of its own. This means that it takes precedence in the minds of many, if not most, Americans in all aspects of the society affecting the life chances of black people. For as Joel Kovel has pointed out, "racism springs from the most widespread and impenetrable level of the American experience."[16] It is no accident that black people in the United States are among the poorest citizens of the society, that they continue to die from diseases easily controlled by modern medical techniques, and that they continue to face racism in all aspects of life.

In his comparative study of race in the United States and South Africa, George Fredrickson makes a strong case for class bias over racial discrimination in both countries. However, he notes the pervasiveness of racism in the United States. There is the case of the race riot in East St. Louis, Illinois, in 1917. One company actively recruited black workers as a means of heading off unionization of the work force. In a strike in which most of the strike breakers were white, ". . . it was the black ones who were remembered by the workers who had lost their jobs."[17]

The class struggle might explain some of the antipathy of whites toward black people in the United States, but it is insufficient to explain race relations. Black people are the victims of oppression because of their racial heritage, not because they are separated from whites by class differences. Indeed, in matters involving the two races upper-class blacks fare no better than do poor blacks. In the eyes of white Americans, race is the salient factor in relations with blacks.

Because of this, it is unlikely that racism is declining in the United States. The most obvious cases of gross discrimination and segregation have somewhat abated, but the basic racism remains. And to maintain that the nation might be headed for class warfare between middle-class blacks and the so-called black underclass ignores the basic historical facts of racism. In Chapter VI, an attempt is made to show that although many middle-class blacks have abandoned the black underclass the animosity between the two groups is hardly sufficient to justify such dire predictions.

Clearly one of the functions of racism is the subjugation of all workers by the ruling class. After the Civil War, for example, it was the policy of some landowners and the owners of factories to employ blacks. However, "every attempt to bring about cooperation on the part of poor whites and landless Negroes was labeled as treason against the white race."[18] In other words, racism (white supremacy) was used to maintain the system of exploitation.

Class and race

Class is an economic concept embracing the whole of society and regulating the behavior of its members. It may control racial minorities in some circumstances, or it may have little or no bearing on race relations. In the United States race has played such a crucial role historically that it is difficult to know which variable is the more salient in black–white relations. Insofar as the life chances of black people are concerned, it must be concluded that racism frequently operates as the single factor directly responsible for their oppression. If a General Motors Plant in Kentucky discriminates against blacks, they cannot be expected to blame corporate officials in Michigan. Their problem is one of earning a living, and although the instructions might come from Michigan, they are implemented on the lower level. Management may have developed the policy, but it was left to the local officials to carry it out.

Race is often utilized as a divisive measure by whites, especially the ruling class. Throughout much of the period after the Civil War whites who owned farms and factories told their white employees that if unionization occurred it would bring integration with it. Because the white employees had accepted the "inferiority" of blacks, they diligently voted to keep unions out of these facilities. In this manner the owners were able to either keep blacks out or keep them segregated. In other words the "unionization means integration" cry served to keep black and white workers both divided and exploited.

It is quite possible, even likely, that with industrialization there was a chance for blacks to become integrated into the larger society, but racism precluded them from taking the path of members of European ethnic groups. In the South after the Civil War violence was the tool used to keep blacks oppressed and to keep them from migrating to the labor markets of the North.[19] Northern employers generally kept blacks out of the labor force or relegated them to menial jobs. But when immigration from Europe was terminated because of World War I these employers were willing to put aside their racist views in an effort to find employees. Indeed, they even went into the South to recruit black labor. But the prosperity of black labor was not to be permanent. Rather, there soon developed a caste system in which menial jobs were reserved for blacks and the higher-status positions were reserved for whites. This practice meant that black workers were not competing for jobs with European immigrants and that there was virtually no possibility of mobility. Racism being an ideology that was accepted even by European ethnic groups, the segregation of blacks at the lowest occupational level became institutionalized. It was not until the beginning of World War II, when the need for workers was at its peak, that Afro-Americans began to break out of the caste system.

There have been movements in the society to somehow come to terms with the oppression of black people, but the racist ideology is so deeply entrenched that it would probably take many decades for this to happen.

The forms of segregation imposed on the black population between the end of Reconstruction and the Civil Rights Act of 1964 were legion. They covered every aspect of life from birth to death. The ideology of racism had become so pervasive that every black person in the country was its victim. The number of black persons murdered simply because of race in this period is unknown, for accurate statistics were not kept. It would no doubt include many thousands.

One crucial aspect of racism in the United States has been that for centuries the law was used to uphold and perpetuate the racism of the society. The proliferation of racist laws over many years reflected the determination to maintain white supremacy in every institution. Two of the most significant judgments occurred in the nineteenth century, one during the antebellum period and the other in the post-Reconstruction period. In 1857, in *Dred Scott v. Sandford*, chief justice of the Supreme Court Roger Taney, writing for the majority, declared that "blacks had no rights which the white man was bound to respect." And in 1896 the Court ruled, in *Plessey v. Ferguson*, that "the argument also assumes that social prejudice may be overcome by Legislation, and that equal rights cannot be secured to the negro except by enforced commingling of the two races. We cannot accept this proposition." The Court concluded "If one race be inferior to the other socially, The Constitution of the United States cannot put them on the same plane." This decision upheld the doctrine of separate but equal. The two decisions simply informed both blacks and whites that segregation was a permanent part of the American way of life.

These judgments and hundreds of laws have left a legacy of black oppression that will no doubt require centuries to eradicate and that continues to impinge on the lives of black Americans. Racism is less overt and less harsh than in previous periods, but it is real and no black person can escape its grip.

In the United States class conflict is much broader than racial conflict, but the two are linked and thrive on each other. Some of the incidents of racial oppression, especially those affecting black people, have a class basis, but they are in a minority. That black people fare less well than, say, European or other immigrants, can be attributed to their race, not their class. In encounters with white people blacks of the same social class level are treated no differently than other blacks. What appears to have happened is that racism, so long a part of the norms of American life, has taken on a life of its own and is not necessarily linked to other ideological strains in the society. It operates autonomously. Racist ideology might have developed during slavery to justify the oppression of blacks, but today the ideology requires no justification. It simply exists.

A recent election demonstrates the racist nature of American society.[20] In the election for the governorship of California in 1982, for the first time a black man, the mayor of Los Angeles, ran for governor on the Democratic ticket. Although California has a large minority population, black voters represent only about 7.5 percent of the electorate. There have been several blacks in the past who succeeded in statewide elections: A black lieutenant governor was elected earlier, as was a black state superintendent of public instruction. Furthermore, the Democrats had a 2:1 ratio of registered voters, and this fact alone should have led to the election of the black candidate for governor. In addition, the candidate was generally considered to be a moderate, well liked by the people of California, and because Los Angeles is a major city he had received national attention as a mayor who served all the people of the city well. Preelection polls uniformly predicted that he would win; less than one month before the election the polls gave him a 13 percent lead. He not only received the endorsement of the major labor unions, but of the state's major newspapers as well. He was considered to be a safe black.

The election campaign of his Republican opponent was not overtly racist, but as is usually the case white voters understood his subtle message. And in November 1982, Los Angeles mayor Tom Bradley was defeated in his bid to become the country's first black elected governor since Reconstruction. He lost the race by a few thousand votes. A pollster conducted an exit poll of voters, asking among other things, for whom they had voted and why. Approximately 4 percent of white voters said they did not want a black governor. This figure translates into 136,000 votes, more than the final plurality for Bradley's opponent.

It is clear that a major issue in this election was race and it was the racism of white voters that kept Bradley from being elected governor of California. This case illustrates that race determines black life chances in the United States. As Robert Staples has written: "They [whites] forfeit their long term class interests for short term racial gains."

Although class is an important variable in all aspects of American life, including the status of black people, race becomes the salient issue in black–white relations. One is reminded of the prophecy of W. E. B. Du Bois at the turn of the century: "The problem of the twentieth century is the problem of the color-line, – the relation of the darker to the lighter races of men in Asia and Africa, in America and the islands of the sea."[21]

IV

WHITE ATTITUDES AND BEHAVIOR TOWARD BLACK PEOPLE

IT is true that prejudiced attitudes frequently translate themselves into discriminatory behavior adversely affecting members of minority groups, but it is also true that prejudiced attitudes do not necessarily result in discrimination and segregation. Prejudice is an attitude, whereas discrimination and segregation are forms of behavior that historically have been employed to maintain the subordinate position of blacks in the society. As an attitude prejudice is less salient in its effects than are its behavioral components, namely, discrimination and segregation. That is, one might hold negative attitudes toward blacks, but unless one is in a position to translate such attitudes into behavior, they might have little effect on members of minority groups. Therefore, negative attitudes toward black people are less important than the behavioral manifestations of racial oppression.

This is not to minimize the importance of prejudice in American society, for it often leads to segregation and discrimination against blacks and other minority groups. It is important to note, however, that there is not necessarily a correlation between attitudes and behavior. For example, poor whites are frequently unrestrained in expressing their negative views about black people, whereas those who are better educated are more reluctant to express such attitudes. Most frequently, however, the people who are better educated are in positions of power in the society. And although they are less likely to verbalize negative feelings, they frequently profit from America's racism.

It is difficult, if not impossible, for a white person living in the United States to be free of racist views. For centuries blacks in the United States have been depicted in all institutions as somewhat less than human, and it is understandable that these views have been internalized by the vast majority of white people. The problem, then, for those who would prefer a more just society is to recognize that they have not been exempted from America's racism and to deal with it openly. For as Robert Blauner has written, "Race and racism are not figments of demented imaginations, but are central to the economics, politics, and culture of this nation."[1]

As we will demonstrate in this chapter, prejudiced attitudes of whites are less entrenched today than they were one or two decades ago. And many of the discriminatory practices have also declined. But it is likely to be centuries before black people reach parity with their white counterparts. This results from centuries of oppression, and from the privileges white people enjoy over black people. Capitalism, at its very core, is exploitative, for it thrives on one group's maintaining dominance over another. As long as American society is based largely on class, it is likely that visible members of minorities will be victims of oppression. That is not to say that racism has disappeared from societies that have become transformed from capitalism to socialism. However, the eradication of capitalism is seen as a necessary, if not sufficient, condition for the elimination of both prejudiced attitudes and discriminatory behavior.

If one watches commercial television in the United States, if one is not acquainted with the society, one is likely to get the impression that black people have already reached parity with whites, for a significant number of commercials contain black people. Or if one makes a tour of the American South, one will notice that black people can be seen in positions that were previously reserved for whites. The schools in the South are in many instances more integrated than those outside the region, and where southerners previously addressed a black man as "boy" they now say "sir" and "mister."

On a recent stopover at the Atlanta airport, a quick reading of the principal newspaper, *The Atlanta Constitution*,[2] provided a good example of how superficially race relations have changed in that city and state. Of the fifty-odd photographs in the newspaper, approximately one-third were of black people, including three of the five syndicated columnists. Although Atlanta has a black mayor and a large black middle class, until fairly recently the only pictures of black people were those who had been arrested for alleged criminal behavior. That Atlanta has many middle-class black people and black elected officials indicates that there have been rather drastic changes in race relations. However, the vast majority of black people in that city have not profited from the Civil Rights Act of 1964.

William Graham Sumner, the early American sociologist, wrote after the Civil War: "The two races have not yet made new mores. Vain attempts have been made to control the new order by legislation. The only result is proof that legislation cannot make mores."[3] What Sumner failed to realize is that legislation can indeed change (or reverse) mores. There have been several instances in which legislation has changed the attitudes and behavior of whites toward blacks.

The Charlotte-Mecklenburg, North Carolina, community, with a school population of 73,000 pupils, provides but one example. From 1970 to 1973 each of the ten senior high schools was closed temporarily because of racial fighting, and the school board staunchly resisted busing. But the federal district judge who presided over the case was firm, and today Charlotte-Mecklenburg has been completely integrated for ten years. Said the judge: "Busing is necessary, legal, cheap, safe, and practical." Pontiac, Michigan, and Tampa, Hillsborough County, Florida, are school districts where desegregation through busing has been accepted after initial turmoil.[4] Indeed, blacks in the United States might have made greater progress if those people whose responsibility it is to enforce the laws had taken firmer action and utilized the power they possessed to enforce the laws. The American people, while reluctant to accept radical changes in institutions, are likely to adhere to the law if it is demonstrated that those who evade the law will face the consequences.

It is not the purpose of this chapter to demonstrate how much progress the black people have made, through the years, in achieving parity with white people. As one reads the results of survey data on attitudes of whites toward blacks, it is well to keep in mind that although some progress has been achieved, much remains to be accomplished. Some will erroneously conclude that because significant changes have taken place in white attitudes toward blacks, the struggle for civil rights is over. The relevant point here is that one might view a glass with water in it as being either half-full or half-empty. Rather than viewing the glass as half-full, we prefer to see it half-empty. That is, our emphasis is not on the amount of progress that has already been made, but on how much remains to be done.

The behavioral manifestations of prejudice – discrimination and segregation – are more critical for black people than the attitudes of white people. If an individual white person in a position of power maintains prejudiced attitudes toward black people, but does not discriminate against them (in employment, for example), then those attitudes are unimportant. If, however, one with such attitudes translates them into discriminatory behavior, this then has an adverse effect on black people. This is not to imply that attitudes are unimportant, for they often determine behavior. The major point here is that black people are less concerned with prejudiced attitudes than they are with concrete behavior.

THE DECLINE IN PREJUDICED ATTITUDES

Several public opinion polling organizations have made longitudinal surveys through time on the attitudes of whites toward blacks. One such organization is the Institute for Social Research of the University of Michigan; another is Louis Harris and Associates of New York City. The Institute for Social Research has released the results of national surveys conducted in 1964, 1968, and 1970.[5] Louis Harris and Associates also conducted national longitudinal attitude surveys in 1963, 1966, and 1978.[6] Both of these organizations surveyed black people as well as whites. However, the primary emphasis here is on white attitudes toward blacks since blacks lack the power to translate their negative attitudes into action against white people. In some cases where the differences between the two groups are significant, data from both groups will be used for comparison.

When asked in 1978 to name the two or three biggest problems facing black people that something should be done about, the respondents in the Harris study differed substantially.[7] White respondents listed them in this order: better job training and education (26 percent), discrimination and the lack of equal rights (16 percent), poor housing (15 percent), unemployment (11 percent), and no real problems (11 percent). Blacks, on the other hand, ranked the biggest problems in a different order: unemployment (43 percent), better job training and education (30 percent), poor housing (28 percent), discrimination and the lack of equal rights (20 percent), and getting promoted to better jobs (18 percent). As can be seen from these data, blacks have a different perception of their plight than do whites. One of the major differences is in the area of unemployment; the difference between the two groups is 32 percent. Similarly, only 1 percent of black respondents indicated that blacks have no real problems, while eleven percent of white respondents agreed. Similarly, 9 percent of all whites interviewed said that blacks expected too much in the form of a handout, while fewer than 1 percent of blacks gave the same response. The assumption must be made that since blacks are the victims in this case, their perception more clearly approaches the reality than that of whites.

Both blacks and whites were asked, in 1978, whether a number of groups and organizations were interested in seeing blacks achieve full equality in the United States.[8] Again the perceptions of blacks differed sharply from those of whites. Invariably whites felt that all the organizations and groups were more interested in full equality for black people than did blacks. Table 4.1 presents the "really interested" responses of blacks and whites.

As can be seen from these data, blacks and whites differ substantially in how they perceive the role of government at all levels in achieving full equality for blacks. Whites are more inclined to think that federal, state, and local governments, the Supreme Court, and the army are concerned about furthering black rights. Black people, on the other hand, feel that government is an important ally for achieving full equality and that the government has not been as diligent in this regard as it should have been.

Before analyzing the changes in white attitudes toward

The decline in prejudiced attitudes

Table 4.1 *Black and white perceptions of organizations and agencies supportive of blacks*

Group or organization	Black (%)	White (%)
The U.S. Army	52	73
Universities and colleges	44	72
Television	43	74
Federal government	39	71
Professional schools	36	62
The U.S. Supreme Court	35	63
Labor unions	33	44
Banks	31	40
U.S. Congress	31	58
Newspapers	29	55
Interfaith organizations	29	43
Large corporations	29	41
The Catholic church	28	39
State government	27	58
Local government	27	48
Small local companies	23	26
Local police	21	36
Local real estate companies	18	25
Jewish groups	18	23
White protestant churches	12	33

Source: Unpublished study from Louis Harris and Associates, "A Study of Attitudes Toward Racial and Religious Minorities and Toward Women" (1978).

black people, let us add a note regarding white attitudes toward interracial contact, as measured by the Institute for Social Research of the University of Michigan in 1970. White respondents were asked four questions designed to measure social distance between the races.[9] When asked whether they would mind if a qualified black person were their superior at work, fully 86 percent said they would not mind. Forty-six percent of respondents said they would not "care one way or the other" if they had small children and these children had black friends. Also, 49 percent of respondents said they would not mind at all if a black family with comparable income and education moved next door. Finally, when asked if they could more easily become friends with a black person with the same education and income or a white person with different education and income, nearly one-half (49 percent) responded that they could more easily become friends with a white person. As these data show, antiblack prejudice is alive and well in America.

Now to turn to changes in white attitudes toward black people as reported by the Harris surveys. Again these questions measure social distance, or white attitudes toward social situations with blacks.[10] As these data show there have been some significant changes in attitudes in the fifteen years between 1963 and 1978. Yet in other cases the changes have not been profound. Respondents were asked whether they would be concerned if a certain situation developed. In 1963 fully 90 percent of whites said they would be concerned if their teenage child dated a black person, and in 1978 the percentage had dropped to 79. Similarly, in 1963 some 84 percent said they would be concerned if a close friend or relative married a black, whereas the figure dropped to 60 percent in 1978. The percentage of whites who would be concerned if a black family moved next door declined from 51 percent in 1963 to 27 percent in 1978. On the question of having a child bring a black child home for supper, in 1963 some two-fifths (42 percent) said they would be concerned, and by 1978 one-fifth (20 percent) gave a comparable answer. In 1963 nearly one-third (32 percent) of whites said they would be concerned if a black person tried on clothes before they did in a clothing store, and by 1978 the figure had declined to 14 percent. On the question of using the same public restroom with blacks, nearly one-fourth (24 percent) expressed concern in 1963, whereas by 1978, 7 percent gave similar responses. It might come as a surprise that in 1963 one-fifth (20 percent) of all whites expressed concern about sitting next to a black person on a public bus and about sitting next to a black person at a lunch counter. By 1978 only 6 percent expressed concern in these two areas.

The Harris surveys measured trends in white stereotypes of blacks.[11] In 1963, some two-thirds (66 percent) of whites felt that blacks have less ambition than whites, and by 1978 the figure had declined to 49 percent. The percentage of whites who felt that blacks want to live off handouts declined from 41 percent in 1963 to 36 percent in 1978. In 1963, some 35 percent of whites felt that blacks bred crime, and by 1978 the figure had declined to 29 percent. The Harris surveys presented two statements dealing with comparative intelligence between blacks and whites. One statement was: "Blacks have less intelligence than whites"; the other was: "Blacks are inferior to white people." The responses demonstrate that a significant segment of white people actually feel that blacks are inferior to whites. On the first statement 39 percent in 1963 said that blacks have less intelligence than whites, and by 1978 the figure had declined to 25 percent. And on the second statement 31 percent in 1963 indicated that blacks are inferior to white people, and by 1978 the figure had dropped to 15 percent. Finally, whites were presented with the statement: "Blacks care less for the family than whites." In 1963, some 31 percent agreed with this statement, and by 1978 the figure was 18 percent.

These figures show that a significant percentage of the white population maintains negative attitudes toward black people. Although there has been a decline in the percentage of whites maintaining stereotypes about black people, these data show that the attitudes of whites toward blacks remain rather strongly negative. To take but one example: It is noteworthy that in 1978, one-fourth of whites continued to feel that blacks have less native intelligence than whites.

Housing has traditionally been one of the areas about which whites have maintained strong feelings in relationship to black people. The last major civil rights legislation affecting black people was the Civil Rights Act of 1968, which deals largely with discrimination in housing. Both the Harris surveys and those of the Institute for Social Research questioned whites about open housing. In the Harris surveys the respondents were asked how they would feel if blacks moved into their neighborhood.[12] In 1963 fully one-half (50 percent) of whites said they would be upset, and by 1978 the figure had dropped to 28 percent. In the University of Michigan surveys respondents were presented with statements about their attitudes toward open housing.[13] In 1964 some 29 percent of respondents said that whites have a right to keep blacks out of their neighborhoods, and by 1970 the figure had diminished to 21 percent. White attitudes on open housing have improved through the years, but it is significant that a sizable proportion of them continues to maintain strongly negative views about open housing.

Both surveys questioned whites on their attitudes toward the pace with which blacks have moved toward full equality. In the Harris surveys they were asked if they felt that blacks have tried to move too fast.[14] In 1963 nearly two-thirds (64 percent) indicated that they felt this was indeed the case. By 1978 the figure had dropped to 37 percent. The University of Michigan surveys focused on the attitude of whites toward the pace with which black leaders were moving.[15] In 1964 more than two-thirds (68 percent) of whites thought that civil rights leaders were pushing too fast, and by 1970 the figure had declined to 57 percent.

Finally, in the University of Michigan surveys whites were asked how they felt about desegregation.[16] Specifically they were asked: "Are you in favor of desegregation, strict segregation, or something in between." In 1964 more than one-fourth (27 percent) indicated that they favored desegregation, and by 1970 the figure was 35 percent. A minority of whites favored strict segregation in both years, and a plurality favored something between strict segregation and desegregation.

These data indicate that the attitudes of white Americans toward blacks have changed substantially in the past few years. These changes have come about since the introduction of civil rights legislation in the 1960s. The data also indicate that in some areas whites still maintain strongly negative attitudes toward blacks. And now we turn to a discussion of discrimination by whites against blacks.

THE PREVALENCE OF RACIAL DISCRIMINATION

Although there has been a decline in prejudiced attitudes toward blacks and some decline in discrimination against them, both remain widespread and account for many of the differences between blacks and whites in income, employment, education, housing, health, and other sectors of the society. As was pointed out earlier, discrimination is not necessarily a direct outgrowth of prejudice, for one may occur without the other. For present purposes, discrimination "refers to actions or practices carried out by members of the dominant groups or their representatives, which have a differential and negative impact on members of subordinate groups."[17] Probably the group in the society most adamant on maintaining the segregation of and discrimination against black people is the Ku Klux Klan, founded during the Reconstruction. There have been several revivals of the secret society and others with the express purpose of maintaining white supremacy. The Klan was founded in Pulaski, Tennessee, in 1866, and has used a variety of techniques to achieve its aims, including lynchings and whippings. It is estimated that during its peak years in the mid-1920s, the Klan enrolled some 4 to 5 million members.[18] During the Depression years of the 1930s, Klan membership dropped to an estimated 30,000. During the civil rights demonstrations of the 1960s, the Klan received new impetus, and since that time it has continued to grow and to attract younger members.

Two of the cities where the Klan has been most active in recent years are Decatur, Alabama, and Tupelo, Mississippi. In 1979 racial animosity surfaced in Decatur when a twenty-five-year-old retarded black man was arrested, tried, convicted, and sentenced to thirty years in prison for allegedly raping three white women. Black demonstrators marched for more than a year, demanding his release, and each time they marched they were confronted by members of the Klan. The protest marches were led by officials from the Southern Christian Leadership Conference, founded by the late Martin Luther King. It should be pointed out that the Klan can no longer expect blacks to tolerate the terror and brutality of its members. This is best illustrated by events in Decatur on May 26.[19] About 100 heavily armed Klansmen attempted to keep seventy-five black demonstrators from marching. The robed Klansmen, armed with clubs, baseball bats, and ax handles, shouted "White Power" and "Niggers, that's as far as you go." They blocked the street and a black man opened fire, causing a fusillade of gunshots. In the ensuing violence two Klansmen and two black demonstrators were injured. Later, in a battle with police and demonstrators half a dozen Klansmen and demonstrators suffered head wounds. No Klansman was arrested in this incident.

The following day, as black demonstrators attempted to march, violence fomented by the Klan again erupted. Again they shouted "White Power! White Power," and carried baseball bats, clubs, and lead pipes. Two Klansmen were injured by gunfire, as were two blacks.[20] Because of the racial violence, ten federal agents went to Decatur to make a case of armed white repression of blacks.

It is estimated that some 2,000 Klansmen were in the area surrounding Decatur. The Imperial Wizard of the Invisible Empire of the Klan, predicting larger turnouts of members at future rallies, gave this as the reason for his optimism: "The Klan 'is the only organization in the United States that's entirely for white people. No matter how you turn it, that's what it comes down to.'" He continued, giving his reasons for the resurgence of the Klan: "The spark that set it off is the government itself," through such policies and programs as affirmative action, school integration, and welfare programs.[21]

In Birmingham, Alabama, a police officer shot in the back and killed a twenty-year-old black woman. This incident precipitated a series of protest marches by blacks and retaliatory violence by the Klan. The Klan and the black demonstrators hurled stones and bottles at each other when blacks gathered to picket the store where the woman had been killed.[22] The mayor of Birmingham refused to dismiss the officer, and no charges were filed.

A black man in Tupelo, Mississippi, was arrested on a bad-check charge while in the company of a white woman. He was jailed in Tupelo and signed a series of confessions, but later maintained that he had been severely beaten by the police. Blacks, in response, conducted a boycott of businesses over several months. The injured black man sued the two police officers involved. The court found the officers guilty of brutality and fined them $2,500 each.[23] Despite the convictions the city refused to dismiss the officers. As a result blacks escalated their protests. They also demanded an affirmative action program to increase minority employment in the city's work force to 30 percent. In addition, demands were made for more black teachers and school administrators and for the upgrading of blacks in the police and fire departments. The Ku Klux Klan threatened to make citizens' arrests of the demonstrating blacks, and at first the city granted permission for such arrests, but the blacks threatened to meet "blood for blood." Finally, a representative of the U.S. Department of Justice persuaded the city officials to rescind their permission for citizens' arrests.

The revival of the Klan is by no means limited to the South. It functions throughout the nation, and is especially strong in the armed forces. In Germany, for example, the Klan is strong among white servicemen.[24] Indeed, an official of the Defense Department has recently reported "a dramatic increase in manifestations of K.K.K. activity" among off-duty service personnel. The official said that she had many reports of white personnel baiting blacks by flaunting KKK-type symbols while in civilian clothes and away from their bases in the United States and West Germany.[25] She placed blame for the increasing Klan activity on what she termed "a new racism" in the military resulting from a misunderstanding of affirmative action programs designed to increase opportunities for minorities and women. The official complained that commanders had become complacent about racial conditions, and she insisted that they become more sensitive to the backlash.

Although members of the Klan are not as likely to terrorize and lynch black people as they once did, the revival of the Klan throughout the country is simply another way of attempting to maintain white supremacy. And although it operates openly in small southern towns and on military bases in Germany, it is not yet a big-city phenomenon. No one knows exactly what the Klan membership is, but it is clear that it is growing in the South and elsewhere. Klan officials conduct nationwide membership drives in an effort to maintain discrimination against blacks.

Housing is one of the areas in which black people have faced greatest discrimination. A South African novelist visiting the United States summed up the housing situation for blacks as follows: "School segregation is dying, but in housing the Negro's dilemma is grim. In most cases they can either live quietly in the slums or dangerously elsewhere."[26] Although

69

the situation is less grim today, housing remains one of the areas of discrimination against black people. Several studies show this to be the case. The Department of Housing and Urban Development published, in 1976, a study of housing for blacks.[27] To the question, "How well are blacks housed?" the answer was "very badly." It continued: "The housing of blacks is more than twice as often physically flawed as is the housing of the total population. And to live in adequate accomodations [sic], a black household must spend a larger proportion of its income in housing than the average householder needs to." This study indicates that in terms of plumbing, kitchen equipment, maintenance, heating, electrical fixtures, sewage and toilet access, nearly 10 percent of all housing in the United States was flawed in 1976, compared with over 21 percent of black housing.

Furthermore, whether blacks rent or own property it is more likely to be flawed than comparable property inhabited by whites. Of all rental units, 17 percent were flawed, compared with 27.7 percent of all black rental units. Slightly more than 4 percent of all owner-occupied units were flawed, while 13.2 percent of all black owner-occupied units were flawed. The explanations given for this situation were discriminatory practices and economic factors.

In a more recent study, conducted for the Department of Housing and Urban Development by the National Committee Against Discrimination in Housing, surveys were made of some forty cities throughout the country. It was found that blacks looking for apartments to rent encounter discrimination three out of four times. And blacks in the market to purchase a house were discriminated against two out of three times.[28] When broken down by geographical location, blacks faced greater discrimination in the north-central region of the country than in other areas. A black person going to a sales office in that region would encounter discrimination 40 percent of the time, and 12 percent in the Northeast, which had the lowest incidence of discrimination. The study utilized black and white checkers who posed as prospective buyers or renters and who visited firms that had advertised in local newspapers.

The Department of Housing and Urban Development has

worked out an affirmative action agreement with the National Association of Realtors. The agreement resulted from continued racial policies of real estate dealers. Although it has not been able to curb discrimination in housing, for violation of fair housing legislation is widespread, the agreement makes it somewhat more difficult for local real estate dealers to discriminate against blacks. And Congress is considering legislation that would strengthen Title VIII of the Civil Rights Act of 1968.

A civic group in Ohio studies discrimination in housing in that state. It was found that 26 of the 136 census tracts in Cuyahoga County, including Cleveland and most of its suburbs, had no nonwhite residents.[29] Such a pattern is similar to the New York City metropolitan area, and others around the country.

Although the discrimination blacks face is less blatant than it was prior to the Civil Rights Act of 1968, and although some attribute discrimination in housing to economic factors, the Urban Institute in Washington, in a recent study, concluded that there was "striking evidence . . . that ghettoization of the nation's blacks is not the direct consequence of their lower incomes." If residence were determined by income, the study concluded, fewer than 1 percent of blacks would live in areas where they are in a majority. At present, because of discriminatory policies, 74 percent of blacks live in census tracts that are more than 50 percent black.[30]

Discrimination in housing is a function of many factors, including broker practices and years of ingrained cultural attitudes. But one of the major causes is the lack of enforcement of the law by the Department of Housing and Urban Development. The department argues, on the other hand, that new laws are necessary to curb this, the most widely practiced form of discrimination.

An example of the difficulty black people face in securing adequate housing comes from Mobile, Alabama.[31] A black man and his family moved into a middle-class, all-white Mobile neighborhood on August 2, 1977. The house had been sold to him by a white woman. In mid-August, while the children were at home alone a brick was thrown through the window. The children looked out and saw two white boys

71

riding away on bicycles. The father later telephoned the police, who maintained that they could do nothing. And a few nights later another brick was thrown through a window, and again the police maintained that they could do nothing. Indeed, a policeman told the black family that they should be living in "Niggerville."

On August 26 someone threw a fire bomb that hit the backyard fence. The police were called and again maintained that they could do nothing. Finally, on Labor Day the occupants were having a family cookout. Many relatives were there, most of them swimming in the pool. A fourteen-year-old son and another teenager borrowed the family car for a short drive to the neighborhood store. The boys had been gone only five minutes when they returned, speeding into the driveway. Before they could leave the car, another car containing two young white men drove into the yard behind them. One white man was wielding a lug wrench, the other a machete. They got out of the car and began chasing the teenagers, who ran screaming to the backyard. One man caught the fourteen-year-old son and started kicking him in the face.

The father, who had been swimming in the pool, went immediately into the house to get his .38 pistol. His father-in-law went to talk with the man with the machete. The father asked what the two white men were doing at his house. The one with the machete dropped it. His twenty-year-old companion picked up the machete and exclaimed: "I am going to kill some of these niggers out here – I am tired of . . ." The father was standing on the porch when he saw the man approaching and swinging the machete. He approached the father, who pulled out his pistol and fired a warning shot. He continued to approach, swinging the machete. When the man refused to stop the father fired two shots in rapid succession, killing the intruder, who still had the machete clutched in his hand. The father was charged with first-degree murder in the death of the intruder.

Such cases as this are far more common than is generally known. Furthermore, although this case happened in Alabama, they occur in all parts of the country, and black families experience difficulty in securing police protection. Many blacks who move into previously all-white neighborhoods find it necessary to arm themselves. State, municipal, and federal laws simply do not curb white violence against blacks who attempt to settle in predominantly white neighborhoods. Two of the most reliable indicators of the quality of life of a people are health and mortality. The black community in the United States more closely resembles a developing nation than a highly industrialized one. If one compares the life expectancy at birth for blacks and whites the difference becomes clear. As of 1974 black males had a life expectancy of 62.9 years compared to 68.9 years for white males.[32] For black women it was 71.2 years, compared to 76.6 years for white females.

The infant mortality rate for white babies was 14.2 per 1,000 live births in 1975, compared to 24.2 for black babies. And the maternal mortality rate for black women exceeded that of white women by three times.[33]

Black people continue to die in disproportionately high rates from diseases easily cured by modern medical techniques. For example, in 1974 the tuberculosis death rate for blacks was four times that of whites. Blacks died of diabetes at a rate of 22 per 100,000 population, compared with a rate of 17 for whites. And hypertension is a major cause of deaths for blacks. When compared with whites, blacks are twice as likely to die from that disease. Finally, blacks are much more likely than whites to die from cirrhosis of the liver, an apparent indication that frustrations encountered by blacks drive them to drink excessively. In 1974 some 20.4 blacks per 100,000 died of cirrhosis of the liver; the corresponding figure for whites was 15.1.[34]

These black–white differentials in deaths from selected diseases result from racial discrimination. If blacks were not the victims of discrimination these differences would not occur. Blacks simply do not have equal access to health care.

The Harlem community in New York City provides a good example of a community of poor residents who receive generally poor medical care. Their health is the worst in New York City. These residents, because of their poverty, are much more likely than others to be the victims of high blood pressure, anemia, obesity, decaying teeth, malnutrition, pneumonia, diabetes, and alcoholism. According to the *New York*

Times, the persistence of such conditions stems from three major sources: inadequate diets and debilitating living conditions in the community's badly heated and maintained housing stock; the unhealthy lifestyle followed by the section's large population of alcoholics, drug addicts, and street people; and the absence of a good system of health care.[35]

Just as black people in the United States exceed white people in death and infant mortality rates, so do the people of Harlem lead New York City in these two indicators of well-being. For example, in 1976 the death rate in central Harlem was 14.5 per 1,000 population, while the citywide rate was 10.2, or nearly 50 percent lower. In the same year the infant mortality rate was 42.8 per 1,000 live births, or more than double the citywide rate of 19.0.[36]

New York City is well provided with doctors, with almost twice the national average. Although the city has an average of about 1.6 doctors for every 1,000 people, Harlem has far less than one doctor for every 1,000 people. Indeed, the 150,000 people in central Harlem are serviced by only fifty doctors, most of whom are old and near retirement. So the people of Harlem are unable to share in the advances of medical technology, and because of the conditions under which they live they are forced to contend with high incidences of ill health and death.

As a consequence of being a powerless minority, black people continue to experience exceptionally high rates of unemployment. Many explanations have been offered for this phenomenon, but in most cases it boils down to a question of discrimination. According to the Department of Labor, the unemployment rate among blacks during 1978 was 12.3 percent, compared to an unemployment rate among whites of 5.4 percent.[37] The jobless rate among blacks is 2.3 times higher than the rate among whites – the widest the gap has ever been. Utilizing what is called the "Hidden Unemployment Index" the National Urban League estimates that the jobless rate in 1978 was 23.1 percent among blacks, and 11.1 percent among whites.[38] It is clear from these data that the unemployment gap between blacks and whites is the widest it has ever been. Since the highest level of unemployment reached during the Great Depression of the 1930s was one-fourth of the nation's labor force, and the black unemployment rate is one-fourth at present, the economic situation in the black community can only be characterized as a depression. If the overall unemployment situation is depressing for blacks, it is grim for black teenagers. The Department of Labor reports that in 1978 the unemployment rate for black teenagers was 38 percent, while the National Urban League (in its Hidden Unemployment Index) reported that approximately three-fifths (57 percent) were unemployed. For white teenagers the unemployment rate in 1978 was 14 percent.[39]

Unemployment among black teenagers is conducive to engaging in illegal activities in an effort to survive. Some of them deal in drugs or engage in other criminal acts such as armed assault, numbers running, and theft. Considering the black teenage unemployment rate, it is not surprising that the crime rate has soared. The rate of black teenage unemployment has increased steadily for the past twenty-five years.

In addition to the plight of black teenagers, other blacks face discrimination in employment. For example, the American Society of Newspaper Editors reports that two-thirds of the nation's newspapers have no black employees, and only 4 percent of the reporters and editors on daily newspapers are members of minority groups.[40] The society reported that of the thousands of editors in top newspaper management, only eleven are members of minority groups. In addition, about one-half of the minority journalists are employed on black newspapers.

The Atlanta-based Southern Regional Council conducted a survey of municipal employment in sixteen southern cities. It was found that these cities either disregard affirmative action programs for blacks and women, or that blacks and women continue to hold low-status, low-paying jobs. The higher-status positions are generally held by white men. In these cities blacks and women represented only 7 percent of all employees earning $13,000 or more.[41] If the present low rate of employment for blacks and women continues it will be at least fifty years before they reach job parity with white males. The study found that even when blacks and women held the

75

same job classification as white men, they were paid lower salaries. Most black employees were to be found in service and maintenance jobs, and women were usually typists. Finally, the United States Supreme Court appears to be a major discriminator against blacks and women. In response to reporters' questions on affirmative action, the Court revealed that most of its workers are white and male, and that there have been only two black law clerks in the Court's history.[42] There have been twenty-two female law clerks. At the present time there are five female clerks and twenty-seven male clerks, all of them white. Each of the Court's justices has a messenger to run errands. All are black except for one who comes from Thailand. And of the eight courtroom attendants, three are black and three are women.

One of the problems facing blacks in general and black teenagers in particular is that of police brutality, or more specifically, police murder. Police kill civilians throughout the country, and blacks, being the most widely dispersed group, are more likely than other minorities to be targets of police killings. In addition to blacks, Native Americans, Chicanos, and Puerto Ricans are frequent targets.

One study of the use of fatal force by the police was conducted in Chicago. This study found that blacks were seven times more likely to be killed by the police than whites.[43] Almost all of the minors killed by the police are members of minority groups, usually blacks. For example, on Thanksgiving Day, 1976, Robert Torsney, a white police officer in Brooklyn, simply walked up to a fifteen-year-old black youth and shot and killed him. He was tried by an all-white jury in Brooklyn and acquitted because a psychiatrist claimed he suffered from some rare form of epilepsy.

The case unfolded in the following manner.[44] Thanksgiving Day, 1976: Robert Torsney fired a fatal shot into the head of fifteen-year-old Randolph Evans. Torsney claimed he was shooting in self-defense: He charged that the boy had a gun. The other officers with him denied that the youth had a gun. November 30, 1976: An assistant district attorney called the killing "totally unprovoked, unjustifiable, and intentional." Torsney was indicted for first-degree murder. November 1977: Witnesses at the trial, including other police officers,

testified that the youth had no weapon and that the officer ̣
him without provocation and seemed calm afterward. Howe
er, Dr. Daniel Schwartz, chief of forensic psychiatry at King
County Hospital, testified that the defendant had suffered a
psychotic episode associated with epilepsy. Schwartz labeled
Torsney insane. November 30, 1977: Torsney was acquitted
for reasons of insanity and was sent to a mental hospital.
December 21, 1978: New York Supreme Court justice Leonard
Yoswein ordered Torsney released from the hospital because
he was "not a danger to himself or others." The judge observed that Torsney did not appear to have been insane at any
time during his committal. Torsney's lawyer commenced
legal proceedings to obtain for his client a $15,000-a-year
police pension on grounds of mental disability.

Then there was the case of the murder of young John
Brabham, a college student, who was murdered by William
Walker, a white policeman. Brabham ran a traffic light in
Brooklyn. He stopped the car, ran, and was pursued by the
officer. The officer claimed that he ordered the youth to
"freeze," an order that was ignored, according to the officer.
Walker said he noticed a pistol in the young man's hand, and
because of this he fired twice. One of the bullets killed the
youth. A toy pistol was found near Brabham's body, and later
testimony by fellow officers indicated that Walker had done
what is so widely practiced in urban areas. He had planted the
pistol beside Brabham's body in order to make it appear that
the youth had a pistol. Officer Walker was acquitted by an all-
white jury. After the verdict the police officer said, "These
mistakes don't happen to white people – there's never been a
case where a black officer shot a white fellow officer by mis-
take or shot and killed a white child by error."[45]

These are but two cases of police murder in New York City.
There have been many dozens in that city, and in only one
case was the officer charged with murder. The United States
Civil Rights Commission listed police misconduct as one of
the South's major problems. The members of the Commission
are no doubt correct, but what about the many unarmed
minority youth outside the region who have been murdered
by police who were then freed by all-white juries?

The city of Boston provides a good example of a northern

American city afflicted with problems of racial discrimination. It is also considered to be a city of culture. And while it made news for several years when the public schools were being integrated, the racism remains.[46] It is a city where blacks are afraid to walk on downtown streets, for many have been attacked. Furthermore, members of Boston's black population say they are made to feel unwelcome in restaurants, at sporting events, and in night clubs. Indeed, they say that the racial climate forces them to plan routes to and from work with extreme care.

There have been a number of racial incidents in recent years. A federal judge ordered that the city's low-income housing be gradually integrated in the spring of 1979. Blacks were being given special consideration in that those who wished to live in previously all-white housing were placed at the top of the waiting list. One young black woman moved into an all-white development only to find that she required twenty-four-hour guards for protection. Someone scratched the word "nigger" on her car and later fire bombed it. As a means of defying the judge's order, antiblack whites moved a 73-year-old white woman into a vacant apartment that might have gone to blacks.

In the short space of five months in 1979 eleven black women were murdered. Although there is no evidence linking the murders to the segregationists, members of the black community feel certain that the police are doing little to solve the crimes.

A black psychiatrist remarked that most of Boston is off-limits to blacks, a situation obtaining in few, if any, large American cities. And the courts have found that a pattern of discrimination so pervasive exists that even the most menial and lowest-paying jobs are reserved for whites.

INSTITUTIONAL RACISM

The National Advisory Commission on Civil Disorders described institutional racism in the United States in its final report. "What white Americans have never fully understood – but what the Negro can never forget – is that white society is deeply implicated in the ghetto. White institutions created it, white institutions maintain it, and white society condones it."[47] Carmichael and Hamilton consider acts of discrimination by the total white community against the black community to constitute institutional racism as opposed to individual acts by whites against individual blacks.[48] What this means is that members of racial minorities are systematically excluded from or relegated to subordinate positions in an activity or function that is considered to be important to the maintenance of the society. Such institutions include the economy, education, health, and the administration of justice.

We have attempted to demonstrate how blacks are discriminated against in the American economy. The earnings of blacks with comparable training and experience are slightly more than half those of white males, they are twice as likely to be unemployed, and when they are employed they generally occupy the lowest-status positions. Thus, in this manner the economy as a social institution discriminates against blacks. Although some writers have maintained that racism in the economy has virtually ended, the data (as we will show) do not support this position. One does not easily eliminate racism in the economy; it has been too deeply rooted for centuries.

In the institution of education, like the economy, members of racial minorities face constant racism. Each year when public schools open, there is massive resistance to the busing of pupils. Indeed, the entire system of education serves as a paternalistic institution for blacks. They are constantly told that they cannot perform as well as whites, and since they are not always taught with the same degree of diligence, the self-fulfilling prophecy operates to prevent them from performing on the same level as white students. Equally important is the widespread procedure of providing better-qualified teachers, better instructional materials, and better physical facilities for schools in white areas.

In the administration of justice one sees institutional racism in its most blatant form. Although black people comprise approximately 11 percent of the population, they account for nearly 50 percent of state prison inmates. They serve longer sentences than whites for the same offense, and capital punishment has been virtually reserved for black men. Any urban black man, and the vast majority live in cities, who

79

reaches the age of twenty-five and has not attended college is likely to have had some encounter with the criminal justice system. And the murder of hundreds of black people (including children) each year by the police illustrates that institutional racism is the norm in the society.

Finally, health care is an area of serious institutional racism. Black people, including infants, continue to die in disproportionately high numbers from diseases that are easily controlled by modern medical techniques. Black people are not provided with information on nutrition, and when they are they are unable to purchase the most nutritious foods. White doctors are not likely to practice medicine in the black community, and insufficient numbers of black students are admitted to medical school. Hence, the community is poorly served in terms of health care.

V

INCOME, OCCUPATION, AND UNEMPLOYMENT

THERE has always been controversy surrounding income, occupation, and unemployment for black people. Data in these areas are often collected by different agencies, utilizing different techniques.* All analysts agree, however, that black–white income differentials are substantial; that blacks tend to be employed in lower-status occupations; and that since World War II the unemployment rate for blacks has been consistently at least twice that for whites. Explanations for these differences depend on the interpretations of the different analysts, and they vary widely. For example, there is some debate over whether a segment of the black population has now reached income parity with its white counterpart. Indeed, the debate has been taken further to include those who maintain that race is no longer a crucial variable in American life.

The data presented here on income, occupation, and unemployment are largely from federal sources. The objective is to compare blacks and whites on these three variables in an attempt to clarify the differences between the two groups.

INCOME

The question of black income compared with that of whites has generated great controversy in recent years. At the beginning it might be useful to review the comments of some writers in this area. Richard Freeman maintains that during the 1960s, "the starting salaries of black college graduates reached parity with those of whites." According to his data, "The income of black college graduates rose sharply relative to that of white graduates, ending the historic pattern of in-

81

creasing racial income differentials with the level of education."[1] He continues: "Black and white occupational distributions tended to converge, as black women moved from
domestic service to factory and clerical jobs and as black men
increased their representation in craft, professional, and
managerial jobs."[2]

Perhaps the most controversial and disturbing report is that
by William Wilson. He contends that "race relations in America have undergone fundamental changes in recent years, so
much so that now the life chances of individual blacks have
more to do with their economic class position than with their
day-to-day encounters with whites."[3] According to his analysis, "Race relations in America have moved from economic
racial oppression to a form of class subordination."[4] Perhaps
the key to his position is stated in the conclusion: "In short,
unlike in previous periods of American race relations, economic class is now a more important factor than race in
determining job placement for blacks."[5] Finally, Wilson
claims that "despite the fact that the recession of the early
1970s decreased job prospects for all educated workers, the
more educated blacks continued to experience a faster rate of
job advancement than their white counterparts."[6]

James Smith and Finis Welch, two economists for the Rand
Corporation, have published a study financed by the National
Science Foundation in which they conclude that "between
1968 and 1975, black male wages have risen at a more rapid
rate than those of whites, continuing a process that occurred
during the 1960s."[7] These authors maintain that blacks and
whites are becoming more alike in the attributes producing
higher wages, and they deny that blacks have been relegated
to dead-end jobs. To their credit, however, they acknowledge
that if the present rate continues, it will take thirty to forty
years for the earnings of black men to reach those of white
men.

The United States Bureau of the Census reported in 1972
that "the young black families (household head under 35) in
the North and West where both husband and wife were earners, had in 1971, achieved income parity with their white
counterparts."[8] It was quickly added, however, that "these

82

Income

young black husband-wife families comprised a relatively small proportion of all black families."

~There is no doubt an element of truth in most of these accounts, but they appear to be premature. As the Census Bureau makes clear, so few black families have reached parity with white families that it can hardly be considered a trend. Recent data demonstrate that in some regards the income gap between blacks and whites is widening rather than narrowing (see Table 5.1). The Bureau of the Census correctly notes: "In summary, significant advances have been made by Black Americans since the first census was taken in 1790. However, in 1978, the 25.4 million Blacks in the country remained far behind whites in almost every social and economic area."[9]

As can be seen from this table the black–white income ratio for families has narrowed somewhat in the past thirty years, going anywhere from slightly more than one-half of that for

Table 5.1. *Median family income, in current dollars, by race, 1950–80*

Year	All families	Black & other	White	Black:white ratio
1950	3,319	1,869	3,445	0.54
1955	4,418	2,544	4,618	0.55
1960	5,620	3,230	5,835	0.55
1965	6,957	3,993	7,251	0.55
1970	9,867	6,516	10,236	0.63
1971	10,285	6,714	10,672	0.63
1972	11,116	7,106	11,549	0.61
1973	12,051	7,596	12,595	0.60
1974	12,902	8,578	13,408	0.64
1975	13,719	9,321	14,268	0.65
1976	14,958	9,821	15,537	0.63
1977	16,009	10,142	16,740	0.60
1978	17,640	11,368	18,368	0.64
1979	19,684	12,358	20,524	0.60
1980	21,023	16,674	21,904	0.58

Source: Adapted from Bureau of the Census, *Statistical Abstract of the United States: 1980;* and Bureau of the Census, *Current Population Reports*, ser. P-60, no. 123, 1982.

whites to nearly two-thirds. For some this might appear to be "great progress," but from the point of view of the black population the gains hardly support the optimistic accounts reported in the literature. It is significant to note that the ratio has fluctuated rather than remained constant. Had the gain been constant there might have been greater justification for these claims of progress. The gap between the races was narrower in 1970 than in 1980. This hardly represents progress.

It should also be noted that the percentage of black females in the labor force exceeds that of whites. For example, in 1977 some 55 percent of black married women with husbands present were in the labor force, compared with 44 percent of white women.[10] In other words, although more members of black families contributed to the family income, they continue to earn considerably less than whites. If the black family contained one earner, however, the income ratio was considerably lower than if there were two or more earners in the family.

Another comparative measure of black–white earnings is the income for persons (see Table 5.2). When these data are examined we find that black women are closer in income to white women than black men are to white men. This is especially true at the higher earning levels. At the same time, both black men and women are disproportionately low earners. In this case black men fare less well than black women.

Since black families on average are larger than white families, they are forced to live on less income, and although some projections envisage a closing of the income gap, these data do not support them. Although fewer white wives worked year round in 1977 than is the case for blacks (33 percent vs. 45 percent), black family income continues to lag behind that of whites. That a higher percentage of white female employees than blacks earn in the lowest income category is probably a function of part-time and seasonal employment on their part.

No analysis of income differentials could be complete without a discussion of poverty. In the United States poverty is not limited to people of color, but as the data show, they are more likely to be its victims than white Americans. Ever since Michael Harrington published *The Other America* in 1962,

Table 5.2. Income of persons – percent distribution by income level, by sex and race, 1980

	Under 2,000	2,000– 3,999	4,000– 5,999	6,000– 7,999	8,000– 9,999	10,000– 12,499	12,500– 14,999	15,000– 19,999	20,000– 24,999	25,000 & over
Male										
Black	14.3	13.7	10.9	9.4	7.9	10.7	7.0	11.2	7.3	7.6
White	8.4	7.3	7.8	7.6	6.7	9.9	7.1	14.6	11.9	18.8
Female										
Black	20.7	24.1	13.5	11.1	7.4	9.4	4.4	6.1	2.1	1.2
White	25.4	17.7	13.2	10.2	8.0	9.1	5.2	6.5	2.6	2.0

Source: Adapted from Bureau of the Census, Current Population Reports, Ser. P-60, Money Income of Households, Families and Persons in the United States, 1980.

haphazard attempts have been made by some administrations, notably that of Lyndon B. Johnson, to ameliorate the problem. Yet what is often called the richest nation in human history has refused to allocate adequate resources for human needs. And in a society whose very structure revolves around the question of race, minorities suffer disproportionately.

When the Bureau of the Census commenced compiling data on poverty in 1959, the percentage of all blacks below the poverty level was 55. That means that more than 9 million of the country's 18 million blacks were classified as poor. This number had dropped somewhat by 1974, but after that the number fluctuated, rising more often than not. The opposite was true for the country's poor whites.

Most poor black families are headed by women, nearly 70 percent of the total. The same is true for poor white families, although the percentage is significantly lower, with fewer than 10 percent of white families classified as poor. Black children are four times as likely to live in poverty than white children, and among the elderly, blacks are twice as likely to be poor as whites. These data are presented in Table 5.3.

These comparative data in large measure demonstrate the wide gap between blacks and whites below the poverty level. It is significant that blacks are more than three times as likely to be poor as whites. Those hit hardest by poverty are the young and the old. More than two out of five black youngsters under the age of fourteen, compared with fewer than 12 percent among whites, a ratio of more than three to one, live in poverty. Among the elderly (sixty-five years and over) blacks are nearly three times as likely to be poor as whites. With data such as these it is difficult to understand claims that race is declining in significance. On many vital indicators the gap between blacks and whites is increasing rather than decreasing.

OCCUPATION

Historically black Americans have been relegated to the lowest levels of the occupational structure. Although this has changed somewhat through the years, they have by no means reached occupational parity with whites. And there has also been a higher proportion of blacks in the labor force. For example, in 1930 the proportion of blacks who were gainfully employed was about ten percentage points higher than whites. But by 1970 the two groups were approximately equal (57 percent).[11] This is largely because black women were much more likely to be employed than white women, especially in domestic service work. For black men the picture is somewhat different. At the end of World War II, nine out of ten black men between the ages of fifty-five and sixty-five were employed, but by 1975 it had declined to seven out of ten.

At the turn of the century virtually all (88 percent) black men worked in agriculture, forestry, fishing, or in domestic service occupations. However, by 1930 the picture changed as blacks moved into unskilled manufacturing and mechanical occupations. As the Bureau of the Census reports, "In each of the census years, 1890 to 1930, the occupational distribution of gainfully employed Blacks differed considerably from that of whites."[12] White workers were more evenly distributed among occupational categories. Discrimination was widespread. In the South blacks were concentrated in agriculture and forestry, whereas those living outside the South were likely to be employed in domestic and personal service jobs.

In 1940 blacks were still concentrated in the lowest-paying, least-skilled occupations, including domestic service and farm positions. As many as one-third of blacks were employed as farm laborers. Twenty years later the proportion had dropped to 8 percent, and by 1970 to 3 percent. On the other extreme, blacks employed in white-collar occupations increased from 6 percent in 1940 to approximately 24 percent in 1970.[13] There has been an upgrading of black workers through the years, but significant differences remain. Whites continue to hold a disproportionate share of the high-status jobs (see Table 5.4). In other words, although blacks have shifted to higher-level occupations, they lag far behind whites. Few blacks are engaged in managerial and professional jobs.

Black women, on the other hand, have made significant gains in white-collar occupations, except at the managerial level. For example, black women working in clerical and sales jobs increased from 1 percent in 1940 to 21 percent in 1970. In the professional categories, lesser gains were made as black

87

Table 5.3. *Persons below poverty level, by age and race, 1981*

	Total			White			Black		
		Below poverty level			Below poverty level			Below poverty level	
Selected characteristics	Total	Number	Percent of total	Total	Number	Percent of total	Total	Number	Percent of total
Age									
Both sexes									
Total	227,157	31,822	14.0	194,504	21,553	11.1	26,834	9,173	34.2
Under 3 years	10,624	2,363	22.2	8,559	1,417	16.6	1,715	857	50.0
3 to 5 years	9,685	2,192	22.6	7,924	1,423	18.0	1,445	690	47.8
6 to 13 years	27,121	5,327	19.6	22,220	3,345	15.1	4,035	1,766	43.8
14 and 15 years	7,190	1,341	18.6	5,940	824	13.9	1,047	464	44.3
16 to 21 years	24,287	3,867	15.9	20,303	2,477	12.2	3,377	1,242	36.8
22 to 44 years	78,828	8,754	11.1	67,675	6,154	9.1	8,921	2,251	25.2
45 to 54 years	22,321	1,914	8.6	19,535	1,306	6.7	2,264	547	24.2
55 to 59 years	11,462	1,060	9.3	10,207	759	7.4	1,030	273	26.6
60 to 64 years	10,408	1,151	11.1	9,351	869	9.3	898	263	29.3
65 years and over	25,231	3,853	15.3	22,791	2,978	13.1	2,102	820	39.0
Total under 18 years	62,449	12,505	20.0	51,140	7,785	15.2	9,374	4,237	45.2
Related children under 18 yrs	62,187	12,324	19.8	50,902	7,624	15.0	9,356	4,223	45.1
Total, 5 to 17 years	45,311	8,682	19.2	37,247	5,403	14.5	6,686	2,932	43.8
Related children 5 to 17 years	45,049	8,501	18.9	37,009	5,242	14.2	6,668	2,918	43.8

Male

Total	110,010	15,560	12.1	94,626	9,100	9.6	12,505	3,744	29.9
Under 16 years	27,908	5,652	20.3	22,882	3,538	15.5	4,157	1,904	45.8
16 to 21 years	12,057	1,707	14.2	10,120	1,099	10.9	1,616	537	33.2
22 to 44 years	38,775	3,373	8.7	33,674	2,515	7.5	4,037	690	17.1
45 to 54 years	10,761	752	7.0	9,484	557	5.9	1,005	168	16.8
55 to 59 years	5,392	385	7.1	4,855	287	5.9	449	85	19.0
60 to 64 years	4,806	411	8.6	4,329	315	7.3	398	87	21.9
65 years and over	10,311	1,080	10.5	9,281	787	8.5	844	272	32.3
Total, under 18 years	31,878	6,276	19.7	26,202	3,932	15.0	4,719	2,116	44.8
Related children under 18 yrs	31,805	6,208	19.5	26,140	3,876	14.8	4,711	2,108	44.7

Female

Total	117,147	18,462	15.8	99,878	12,453	12.5	14,329	5,429	37.9
Under 16 years	26,712	5,570	20.9	21,760	3,472	16.0	4,085	1,873	45.9
16 to 21 years	12,229	2,160	17.7	10,183	1,378	13.5	1,760	705	40.1
22 to 44 years	40,053	5,381	13.4	34,001	3,638	10.7	4,884	1,561	32.0
45 to 54 years	11,561	1,162	10.1	10,051	749	7.4	1,260	378	30.0
55 to 59 years	6,070	676	11.1	5,352	472	8.8	581	188	32.4
60 to 64 years	5,602	740	13.2	5,021	554	11.0	500	176	35.2
65 years and over	14,921	2,773	18.6	13,510	2,191	16.2	1,258	547	43.5
Total, under 18 years	30,571	6,229	20.4	24,938	3,854	15.5	4,654	2,120	45.6
Related children under 18 yrs	30,382	6,116	20.1	24,762	3,748	15.1	4,645	2,115	45.5

Source: Adapted from Bureau of the Census, Current Population Reports, ser. P-60, *Money Income of Households, Families and Persons in the United States, 1981.*

Table 5.4. *Employed persons, percent distribution, by occupation and race, 1960–80*

Occupation	White					Black and other				
	1960	1970	1975	1979	1980	1960	1970	1975	1979	1980
Total employed (1,000)	58,850	70,182	75,713	86,025	86,380	6,927	8,445	9,070	10,920	10,890
Percent	100.0	100.0	100.0	100.0	100.0	100.0	100.0	100.0	100.0	100.0
White-collar workers	46.6	50.8	51.7	52.5	53.9	16.1	27.9	34.7	37.9	39.2
Professional, technical, and kindred[a]	12.1	14.8	15.5	15.9	16.5	4.8	9.1	11.4	12.2	12.7
Medical and other health	2.1	2.3	2.5	2.9	3.0	.8	1.6	2.7	2.7	2.9
Teachers, except college	2.6	3.2	3.6	3.3	3.3	1.7	2.9	3.1	2.9	2.9
Managers and administrators, exc. farm	11.7	11.4	11.2	11.6	12.0	2.6	3.5	4.4	5.2	5.2
Salaried workers	5.9	8.4	9.0	9.6	9.9	.9	2.1	3.4	4.3	4.3
Self-employed	5.8	3.0	2.2	2.0	2.1	1.7	1.4	1.0	1.0	.9
Salesworkers	7.0	6.7	6.9	6.8	6.8	1.5	2.1	2.7	2.8	2.9
Retail trade	4.1	4.0	3.8	3.5	3.4	1.0	1.6	2.0	1.7	1.9
Clerical workers	15.7	18.0	18.1	18.2	18.6	7.3	13.2	15.7	17.7	18.4
Stenographers, typists, and secretaries	3.9	4.7	5.4	5.1	5.2	1.4	2.3	3.4	3.9	3.9

Blue-collar workers	36.2	34.5	32.4	32.6	31.1	40.1	42.2	37.4	36.7	35.8
Craft and kindred workers[a]	13.8	13.5	13.4	13.8	13.3	6.0	8.2	8.8	9.4	9.6
Carpenters	1.4	1.1	1.2	1.4	1.3	.4	.7	.6	.6	.6
Constr. craftworkers, exc. carpenters	2.7	2.5	2.7	2.8	2.7	1.6	1.8	2.1	2.3	2.4
Mechanics and repairers	3.2	3.7	3.6	3.7	3.5	1.7	2.6	2.1	2.4	2.5
Metalcraft workers, except mechanics	1.8	1.6	1.4	1.4	1.4	.6	.8	.8	1.9	1.0
Blue-collar supervisors, n.e.c.	1.9	2.0	1.7	1.9	1.8	.4	.9	1.0	.9	1.2
Operatives	17.9	17.0	14.6	14.4	15.5	20.4	23.7	20.0	19.9	19.4
Operatives, except transport	—	—	10.9	10.8	10.1	—	—	15.0	15.1	14.5
Transport equipment operatives	—	—	3.7	3.6	5.4	—	—	5.0	4.8	4.9
Nonfarm laborers	4.4	4.1	4.4	4.5	4.3	13.7	10.3	8.7	7.4	6.9
Service workers	9.9	10.7	12.3	12.0	12.1	31.7	26.0	25.8	23.2	25.1
Private household workers	1.7	1.3	1.0	.8	.8	14.2	7.7	4.9	3.3	3.2
Service workers, exc. private household	8.2	9.4	11.3	11.1	11.3	17.5	18.3	20.9	19.9	19.9
Farm workers	7.4	4.0	3.6	2.9	2.9	12.1	3.9	2.6	2.2	1.8
Farmers and farm managers	4.3	2.4	2.0	1.6	1.7	3.2	1.0	.6	.3	.3
Farm laborers and supervisors	3.0	1.6	1.5	1.2	1.2	9.0	2.9	2.0	1.9	1.5

[a]Includes occupations not shown separately.

Source: Bureau of the Census, *Statistical Abstract of the United States, 1981.*

women in these occupations increased from 4 percent in 1940 to 10 percent in 1970. These changes resulted from a decline in domestic service work. In 1940 fully 60 percent of black female employees worked as private household workers, whereas this proportion had decreased substantially by 1980.[14]

In certain professional occupations blacks lag far behind whites. By 1970 blacks represented only about 2 percent of physicians and surgeons, and 1 percent of all lawyers and judges. And they constitute about 8 percent of all teachers. Periods of economic recovery and growth are not shared equally by blacks and whites.

If one takes the four major occupational categories – white collar, blue collar, service, and farm workers – there have been major changes between 1960 and 1980. The proportion of blacks in white-collar occupations more than doubled in this period. Blacks still lag considerably behind whites, however. Within this category they have especially lagged behind whites as managers and administrators, positions that are high in both status and pay.

The proportion of blacks in blue-collar occupations declined between 1960 and 1980, due largely to the decline in nonfarm laborers. In the category of service workers, the proportion of black workers is double that of whites. Indeed, as one goes down the occupational ladder to jobs low in prestige and pay, blacks predominate over whites. Private household work has virtually always been the domain of blacks, and as Table 5.4 shows, fewer than 1 percent of whites are engaged in this work in contrast to 3.2 percent for blacks. And for the category of service workers, except private household, again the black proportion is twice that of whites. Approximately one-fifth of all black workers are engaged in this type of service work.

Few Americans are employed as farm workers today, and blacks who are so employed are likely to do the unskilled work, rather than working as managers and supervisors.

In 1979, the National Urban League, in its *The State of Black America 1979* report, had this to say: "The income gap between blacks and whites is actually widening and not only is black unemployment at its highest level in history, but the jobless gap between whites and blacks is also the widest it has ever been." The report continued: "Life for most black Americans instead of being comparatively comfortable – as the misconception would have it – is in fact quite difficult, and in all too many instances is reduced to a matter of basic survival." Commenting on the unemployment rate among blacks, the report continued: "Unemployment in Black America, including those who have given up looking for work and those who hold part-time jobs because they cannot find full-time employment, is 23.1 percent, or roughly one out of every four workers."[15]

The Bureau of the Census has compiled data on the relative unemployment rates for blacks and whites since 1948. These data are published in Current Population Reports, and they show that the black unemployment rate, with few exceptions, has remained at least double that for whites. The exceptions were in the late 1940s and the early 1950s, when the rate was slightly less than double, and also for three years in the 1970s. Since 1948 the unemployment rates for blacks were lowest during the Korean War. After the war, however, the rates began to rise.[16] The rate remained more than double through most of the 1970s. The highest official rate for blacks was 14.9 percent, recorded in 1980, while the highest rate ever recorded for whites was 7.8 percent in 1975. In 1977 the black unemployment rate was 2.4 times the white rate.

In 1980 unemployment rose for both black and white workers. The rate for blacks increased by 2.8 percentage points to 14.9. At the same time the white rate increased from 5.2 to 6.7 percent.[17] It should also be noted that the unemployment rate for blacks is increasing in the 1970s and 1980s at a rate faster than ever before. In 1980, fully 20 percent of unemployed workers were black. And the figures for the beginning of 1981 were not encouraging (Table 5.5).

The Bureau of Labor Statistics categorizes certain workers as "discouraged." These are persons who are not seeking employment because they do not feel they can find it. Although these people are not working they are not counted in the unemployment statistics because they have not searched for work as recently as four weeks prior to being surveyed.

Table 5.5. *Unemployed persons by marital status, race, age, and sex*

	Males (thousands)		% Unemployed		Females (thousands)		% Unemployed	
	Jan. 1980	Jan. 1981	Jan. 1980	Jan. 1981	Jan. 1980	Jan. 1981	Jan. 1980	Jan. 1981
Total, 16 & over	3,933	4,973	5.6	8.3	3,110	3,570	7.1	8.0
Married, spouse present	1,656	2,001	4.1	5.0	1,364	1,631	5.6	6.5
Widowed, divorced, or separated	392	534	8.3	10.4	597	713	7.1	8.2
Single, never married	1,884	2,439	18.0	16.4	1,748	1,226	10.3	10.9
White, 16 & over	3,140	4,066	5.9	7.6	2,391	2,805	6.3	7.2
Married, spouse present	1,427	1,738	3.9	4.8	1,163	1,428	5.3	6.4
Widowed, divorced, or separated	258	426	6.7	10.1	440	529	6.5	7.6
Single, never married	1,445	1,902	11.6	14.8	783	848	8.3	9.0
Black & other, 16 & over	793	907	12.5	14.1	720	765	12.2	12.7

Married, spouse present	230	262	6.4	7.4	197	203	7.6	8.0
Widowed, divorced, or separated	154	108	15.4	11.7	157	184	9.7	10.9
Single, never married	430	536	23.1	26.8	365	378	21.6	21.2
Total, 20–64	3,059	3,905	6.8	7.3	2,382	2,839	6.2	7.1
Married, spouse present	1,572	1,940	4.1	5.1	1,259	1,520	5.3	6.5
Widowed, divorced, or separated	571	521	8.3	10.7	571	669	7.4	8.3
Single, never married	1,092	1,444	10.9	13.8	553	650	7.6	8.5
White, 20–64	2,413	3,219	5.1	6.7	1,829	2,213	5.5	5.4
Married, spouse present	1,355	1,689	3.9	4.9	1,074	1,328	5.1	5.1
Widowed, divorced, or separated	242	417	6.7	10.5	416	489	6.7	7.6
Single, never married	817	1,113	9.5	12.4	389	396	5.7	6.3
Black & other, 20–64	621	685	10.9	11.8	554	627	10.4	11.5
Married, spouse present	217	251	6.8	7.4	184	192	7.4	7.7
Widowed, divorced, or separated	129	104	15.8	11.9	154	180	10.1	11.2
Single, never married	274	332	19.3	21.8	215	254	16.8	18.4

Source: Bureau of Labor Statistics, *Employment and Earnings,* February 1981.

Not only are blacks of all ages more likely to be unemployed than whites, but unemployed blacks are more likely to remain so for an extended period of time. For example, in 1975 fully one-third of all unemployed blacks were without work for at least fifteen weeks, compared with 31 percent of white unemployed workers.[18]

Several explanations have been advanced for the high and expanding unemployment rate among blacks. It is said that more black workers have joined the labor market than could possibly be absorbed. In addition, it is said that black workers are concentrated in the lower-skilled, lower-paying jobs characterized by a higher rate of turnover and a greater incidence of unemployment. And black workers continue to face racial discrimination. Given the nature of American society it is likely that discrimination plays a major role in black unemployment. Robert Hill of the National Urban League explains black unemployment largely in racial terms: "High levels of black unemployment are mainly due to the unavailability of jobs to blacks rather than their unsuitability for these jobs. And the lack of jobs available to blacks is a result of racial discrimination, depressed economy and ineffective targeting."[19]

Discrimination in employment can be seen when jobs requiring little skill go to whites rather than to blacks. In periods of economic growth blacks still retain high rates of unemployment. And blacks, when employed, advance less rapidly than whites in comparable positions. In other words, discrimination is the most salient factor in black unemployment. As one group of writers has noted: "The heart of the [black unemployment] problem lies, not in the size of the GNP [Gross National Product] or the Dow Jones Average, but in discriminatory practices and the lack of effective machinery to deal with them."[20]

Although there have been several legislative acts and executive orders aimed at ending employment discrimination against blacks since World War II, these have failed to end the practice because of weak or nonexistent enforcement.

In addition to the economic burdens of unemployment on blacks, they are affected in other ways. One of these is the loss of self-esteem. It makes it difficult for the husband to support his family, and frequently he takes the easiest way out by leaving the family to be supported by public assistance. Hence, the high percentage of black families headed by females.

We may now evaluate the assumptions enumerated at the beginning of this chapter. Freeman's assertion that black and white occupational distributions tended to converge in the 1960s is not supported by data from the 1970s and 1980s. Indeed, as indicated in Table 5.4, a wide gap in occupational distribution remains, especially for the higher-status, higher-paying jobs. It is at the very lowest levels of the occupational structure that the similarities are greatest.

It is difficult to understand the position of William Wilson. All studies show that racism was on the decline in the 1960s and 1970s, but to assert that the country has moved from economic racial oppression to class subordination simply is not justified by the data. Class is obviously an important variable in a capitalist society, but in the United States race is still the critical variable for black people. As is indicated in Table 5.1, as late as 1979 blacks earned three-fifths as much as their white counterparts.

A study of black economic development delineates some of the ways racial discrimination affects black people.[21] Blacks are taxed on the same basis as whites but are not accorded the same representation in government, nor are blacks provided the same services for which they pay taxes. Frequently, blacks are deprived of their land and homes in order to further the interests of whites, such as highway development and urban renewal. Finally, they are guaranteed certain rights by the Constitution, but are often beaten, jailed, or killed if they exercise these rights.

Smith and Welch maintain that black males' wages have risen at a more rapid rate than those of whites. Table 5.2 shows this not to be the case, and this table, in which the data are divided by sex, also shows that in all the higher income categories white males earn considerably more than blacks.

These notions are far from the reality, and the likelihood is

97

that the gaps in income, occupation, and unemployment are likely to widen, in a society that turned sharply to the right in the 1980 election. One of the outcomes of this shift is that racial prejudice is considerably more fashionable than it was in the preceding two decades.

THE BLACK MIDDLE CLASS

THE black middle class has been, and continues to be, a subject of interest to sociologists and others who have elected to research and write about Afro-Americans. But defining the middle class has been a topic of some controversy. Generally, however, education, income, and occupation are considered to be the three variables by which one's social class may be measured. These three variables are interrelated, although it is possible to use any one as an indicator of social class. Data on these three variables are regularly published by federal agencies, which makes the definition of middle class amenable to statistical measurement, but there is little consensus in sociological literature on the proportion of black families who are middle class.

Since the advent of the civil rights movement many claims have been made about black progress and the rapidity with which blacks have surged into the American middle class. One of the first efforts here will be to review some of the definitions of middle class as the concept relates to blacks and to attempt to arrive at a definition that can be verified utilizing quantitative data.

DEFINING THE BLACK MIDDLE CLASS

The noted sociologist and pioneer in research on the black middle class, E. Franklin Frazier, felt that because of the nature of American society a definition of the black middle class must include those occupying white-collar positions as well as those employed as artisans and supervisors. Those occupations comprising middle-class status include professional and technical workers; managers, officials, and pro-

99

prietors; clerical and sales workers; artisans and supervisors. Frazier found that in 1950 slightly more than 16 percent of all black male workers held such occupations.[1] He maintained that style of life was as important in the black community as, say, income. According to Frazier, a key element in black middle-class life was the notion of respectability. More recently, sociologist William Wilson has utilized Frazier's occupational categories to justify his conclusion that "24 percent [of black males] held such [middle-class] jobs in 1960 and 35.3 percent in 1970."[2] Wilson attempts to support his point that "the life chances of blacks have less to do with race than with economic class affiliation."[3]

Perhaps the most outrageous position is that taken by Wattenberg and Scammon. They report that

> a remarkable development has taken place in America over the last dozen years: for the first time in the history of the republic, truly large and growing numbers of American blacks have been moving into the middle class, so that by now these numbers can reasonably be said to add up to a *majority* of black Americans – a slender majority, but a majority nevertheless.[4]

Utilizing occupational categories alone, these authors include in their definition of black middle class such positions as "plasterers, painters, bus drivers, lathe operators, secretaries, bank tellers, and automobile assembly line workers." Such a distortion of reality, for whatever reason(s), has led Robert B. Hill, a black sociologist with the National Urban League, to write: "It is clear that Wattenberg and Scammon were determined that if they could not get enough blacks *up* into the middle-class, they would bring the middle-class *down* to the blacks!"[5]

Hill feels that the term "middle income" is more appropriate than "middle class" because policy makers use the term to delineate economic classes rather than social classes. According to Hill, 1975 data from the Bureau of Labor Statistics reveal that about 23 percent of all black families were "middle-income," in contrast to 46 percent of all white families.[6] These data are based on the bureau's Standard Budget Level figures in which a family income of $15,318–$22,294 is considered to be intermediate. Based on these data Hill reveals that there

100

was not a significant increase in the proportion of black families who are middle class between 1972 and 1976. Indeed, he finds that the proportion of such families decreased by two percentage points between 1972 and 1975.

In an article on the black middle class, appearing in the *New York Times Magazine,* the author reports that in 1976 some 21 percent of black families were middle class.[7] This assertion is based on census data revealing that slightly more than one-fifth (21 percent) of black families had incomes between $15,000 and $24,999 in 1976. However, his definition of middle class, based solely on income, is anywhere between $12,000 and $30,000 annually.

Finally, an article in the *Wall Street Journal,* again utilizing Census Bureau data, defines as middle class any family with an annual income of $15,000 or more. Accordingly it is estimated that in 1978 some 36 percent of all black families were members of the middle class.[8] At the same time some 62 percent of all white families earned incomes within the middle-class range.

These definitions of middle class, relying largely on income, utilize family income figures beginning from $12,000 to $15,000, with a maximum family income anywhere from slightly more than $22,000 to those earning in the hundreds of thousands. Other researchers utilize occupational status rather than income. Since these two variables are highly correlated, the results are not unduly different, that is, if one uses white-collar occupations. Education, which is generally correlated with income and occupation, is rarely used in measuring black middle-class status. However, several of the writers make a point of indicating that the black middle class is likely to increase because of the increasing numbers of blacks attending college. As one put it: "Black enrollment in colleges rose an amazing 275 percent between 1966 and 1976, from 282,000 students to 1,062,000."[9] And another: "Brightening prospects for a future increase in the black middle class is the number of blacks going to college: In 1979, 20 percent of all black youths were enrolled there, up sharply from 7 percent in 1960 and just 5 percent in 1950."[10] What these writers fail to report is that a significant proportion of blacks in postsecondary education are enrolled in community colleges, from which they rarely transfer to schools offering baccalaureate degrees. This development is likely to widen the gap between black and white income.

The confusion over defining the black middle class was compounded somewhat by James E. Blackwell in his recent book on the black community.[11] Utilizing a model in a previous work, he reports that the black community is stratified into three classes, with 10 percent of all blacks being in the upper class, 40 percent in the middle class, and 50 percent in the lower class. According to this analysis the black middle class comprises three components: upper middle class professionals, middle-class, white-collar and clerical workers, and skilled blue-collar workers. He sees the upper middle class as those earning between $13,000 and $15,000, with the middle group earning between $9,000 and $13,000, and the skilled blue-collar workers earning between $7,500 and $12,000. Although Blackwell admits that, "their status, like that of those in the upper-class levels, is higher than it would be in the white community," there can be no justification for inflating the size of the black middle class. In 1975, no family, black or white, with an income of $7,500 could legitimately be considered middle class.

According to 1977 census data some 21 percent of all black families earned annual incomes between $15,000 and $24,999, which would place these families in the middle class.[12] (An additional small fraction, some 9 percent, earned $25,000 and over.) At the same time, some 23 percent of all black men held white-collar occupations.[13] Thus, it seems fair to say that somewhere between 20 and 25 percent of all black families and individuals could be said to be middle class. This appears to be a more realistic assessment of the class structure of the black community than the figures presented by some of the more optimistic accounts.

In the same year (1977) 17.2 percent of all black persons in the United States had completed at least one year of college, with more than one-half (9.9 percent) of these having completed between one and three years.[14] At the same time 28.4 percent had completed high school. It is difficult to know the precise extent to which education is correlated with income and occupation in the black community, but it is safe to say that those black persons with some college education are likely to be middle class, whereas some of those with high school diplomas who earn sizable salaries from white-collar occupations may also be so classified.

Most news accounts of middle-class blacks give the impression that the percentage entering that status is swelling. But census data do not support these reports. For example, census data indicate that the proportion of black families earning between $15,000 and $24,999 decreased by one percentage point between 1976 and 1977.[15] And, according to data from the Bureau of Labor Statistics, the proportion of black families in the intermediate income range (middle class) declined from 26 percent in 1972 to 23 percent in 1975.[16] There is no empirical evidence to support the claim that black middle-class families are rapidly increasing in numbers. Given the present political climate, with the aversion of individuals in power to affirmative action in employment, we may expect a continued decline in the number of middle-class black families.

It should be added that one of the significant differences between black middle-class families and their white contemporaries is that in the former a far greater proportion of wives is in the labor force than in the latter. And it is maintained that in certain sections of the country (North and West) young (husband under 35) black husband-wife families reached income parity with comparable white families in 1969.[17] Although these data, which have been widely circulated, impressed many, they accounted for a very small proportion (6 percent) of all black families at the time.

BLACK MIDDLE-CLASS LIFESTYLES

Stephen Birmingham, the chronicler of the very rich of various ethnic groups, has written a somewhat unflattering and condescending book on what he calls the "black upper crust." Among other things he has this to say about the lifestyles of rich black people: "Certain details of behavior, certain 'social graces,' that come naturally to upper-class whites either elude the blacks or, when they try to employ them, seem stilted, forced, and – to a white's way of thinking at least – in poor taste." He continues: "Dressing well, being well groomed, owning your own home and car, and having an education – these are the main criteria for status in black America."[18]

Whereas Birmingham writes about wealthy blacks, E. Franklin Frazier concentrates largely on middle-class blacks in his scathing critique, *Black Bourgeoisie*. His analysis of what he calls the "new middle class" is severe. For example, he feels that the black bourgeoisie has developed feelings of inferiority because of its rejection by the white world and its having rejected the black masses. "In order to compensate for this feeling of inferiority, the black bourgeoisie has created in its isolation what might be described as a world of make believe." He feels that their "emotional and mental conflicts arise partly from their constant striving for status within the Negro world, as well as in the estimation of whites."[19] Frazier is most harsh when he discusses the lifestyles of his subjects. "Although they may pretend to appreciate 'cultural' things, this class as a whole has no real appreciation of art, literature, or music." Elsewhere: "The decor of their homes reveals the most atrocious and childish tastes. Expensive editions of books are bought for decoration and left unread." Finally, he sees poker as their most important form of recreation: "In fact, poker is more than a form of recreation; it is the one absorbing interest of Negro 'society.'"[20] There is no doubt that Frazier's assessment is, in large measure, accurate; however, the book was researched and written in the 1950s, long before the advent of the civil rights movement and before the enforcement of civil rights laws desegregating most aspects of American life.

Another writer, with a more sympathetic attitude toward the black middle class, has this to say: "They can be seen in Bloomingdales, Marshall Field, Nieman-Marcus; in glitzy restaurants, health clubs, tennis courts, theaters and bookstores. They have evolved and assimilated, and retained only one characteristic, besides their blackness: that of having made it and confident they can keep it."[21] This writer prepared a lengthy article on the black middle class, apparently interviewing several of its members. It is significant, however, that he focused on two black females with serious personal or family problems.

Black middle-class lifestyles

His first subject, Rachel Simmons, encounters two black youths attempting to rob a white man on a Chicago subway platform. She manages (like Wonder Woman) to avert the robbery by shouting, "Get the Hell out! You're just continuing the stereotype!" Rachel, a former call girl, works as an advertising agency receptionist; her sister is a prostitute and she has two brothers in prison. Her mother had ten children, "mostly by different men," and her life has been spent on welfare. In Detroit we meet Geri Wagner, who works as an industrial relations manager for a large corporation in Fort Wayne, Indiana. She is in Detroit for, among other things, a visit to Jackson, Michigan, where her brother "is a number on the grounds of Jackson State Prison."

Rachael Simmons, we are told, has "little patience" for her brothers and sisters left behind on the South Side. She is much more interested in her fancy apartment on the North Side, Mercedes Benz automobiles, expensive department stores, and drinking white rum and soda. She considers herself to be assimilated into the American middle class, but on her way to a tavern in her neighborhood one evening she is in for a rude awakening. Suspected of being a prostitute, she is arrested and thrown into an unmarked police car. If there is a moral to Rachael Simmons's story it is that, in the United States, race is more important than class. It is unlikely that her white counterpart would have had to spend a night in jail under comparable circumstances.

Unlike previous periods in American history social mobility for black people is considerably more real; data indicate that the middle-class black community is enlarging itself, perhaps not to the extent that some writers maintain, but it is undeniable that significantly more blacks can now be considered middle class than at any previous period. Far more black people attend college and greater opportunities await them upon graduation. As they become middle class they desperately emulate the behavior of middle-class whites, frequently forgetting their humble backgrounds. Most of them associate socially with other middle-class blacks, either because they have been rejected by whites or because they fear rejection. Unlike Frazier's black bourgeoisie, who, because of rigid racial segregation, were forced into special occupations and neighborhoods, and who were forced to attend all-black colleges, today's middle-class blacks can be found in integrated settings throughout the society. Their lifestyles tend to be similar to those of comparably situated whites, but they frequently exaggerate these, especially in automobiles and clothes. And their blackness means that they will continue to live marginal lives in a deeply racist society.

PROBLEMS OF RACE

In interviews with twenty middle-class blacks in Philadelphia a reporter for the *Wall Street Journal* found that racism was a persistent problem in that city and its suburbs.[22] As a psychologist put it, "Middle class or not, I get watched when I walk into a department store, and I still have to cash my check at a bank that knows me." A school teacher: "My physician is white, and you should see the stares I get when I'm in his waiting room. The whites act like they think I'm going to clean the place when they leave. They think all blacks go to clinics." On the matter of housing discrimination, these middle-class blacks reported that, no matter how much they earn, they are steered by real estate brokers to five or six areas when they shop for an apartment or a house. One informant said he was warned about the possibility of being "burned out" when he asked to be shown a home in one section of the city.

The Census Bureau reports that between 1970 and 1977 the number of blacks living in the suburbs increased by 34 percent.[23] But a move to the suburbs can bring terror for black people as fire bombings and shootings continue. Since federal fair housing laws were enacted in 1968, middle-class blacks have moved to the suburbs in larger numbers than ever before, but the enforcement of these laws has been lax. Consequently, many black families who have purchased houses have been prevented from moving in because of racist terror or threats. In recent years, a black college teacher's home in Chicago was fire bombed and vandalized; crosses were burned at black suburban homes around the country; rocks were thrown through windows and arson was attempted at a black home in Cleveland Heights; a vacant home was burned in New Jersey when rumors were spread that a black family

106

had bought it; in Rockaway, New York, a duplex was set afire nine times in a single year.[24] Such practices are likely to continue as long as American society remains stratified along ethnic lines. And though there is some amelioration in this regard, it is reasonable to assume that racism will remain a factor in American life for the indefinite future.

The United States Commission on Civil Rights concluded that *"discriminatory mortgage lending practices have restricted the home ownership opportunities of middle-income minorities and women, thereby subjecting them more often to higher housing costs and inferior housing and denying them a principal means of saving and accumulating wealth."*[25]

Members of the black middle class may possess the same degree of education, the same income, and the same occupational status as whites, but they are still considered black first and middle class second. Therefore, many associate with one another out of choice, but many also are prohibited from joining the social clubs of whites. There exist, throughout the country, many private clubs that discriminate against minorities and women. It is in these clubs that many political and corporate decisions are made. There are even cities in the country with black mayors who are not permitted to join or attend these private clubs. The black middle class, consequently, continues to rely on friendship cliques, social service clubs, and fraternities and sororities to a greater extent than do their white counterparts.

Although Frazier's study was completed at a time when racial segregation and discrimination were pervasive in the society, many of his characterizations apply to the black middle class of today. This is especially true for the racism confronting blacks who have attained middle-class status. Indeed, as Frazier pointed out, the standards of behavior and values of the black bourgeoisie came into existence "as a consequence of racial discrimination and racial segregation."[26]

Racial discrimination in housing is not limited to members of the black middle class. It affects wealthy blacks as well. This is the area of American society about which white persons are most intransigent, and it is one of the areas where social class plays only a minor role.

The black middle class

The following incident, involving one of the greatest basketball players of all time, illustrates the difficulty even rich blacks have moving into neighborhoods that are totally white. Oscar Robertson, voted one of the five best basketball players of all time, lives in Cincinnati, Ohio. He was considering purchasing a house on the city's most prestigious street, but its residents would not tolerate a black neighbor, not even one who was internationally known (he was co-captain of the American Olympic basketball team that won a Gold Medal) and wealthy. "In the end, the problem resolved itself when Robertson decided against the property and bought a house in another part of town."[27]

If one visits blacks in the wealthy suburbs of many American cities there is almost certain to be a discussion of some form of harassment from their white neighbors. They fear that neighbors and white vigilante groups will fire bomb their homes or otherwise cause personal or property damage. This suspicion is not paranoia, but is based on the large number of such incidents that one reads about almost daily. Given the conservatism sweeping the country, with its heavy dose of racism, there is every indication that such shootings and fire bombings will continue, for they are fueled by individuals at the highest levels of government and some of the so-called religious leaders. In other words, these individuals have created a climate in which expressions of racist sentiment thrive.

Middle-class black travelers, while facing fewer problems than in the past, are still subjected to discrimination and insults. A black journalist and her husband were visiting in New York from Chicago. When a white maid entered the hotel room she was overheard to say, "I guess they let anybody in here these days."[28] And black people are frequently given undesirable rooms like those near elevators or in dark corners.

The occupational positions held by most members of the black middle class since the second half of the 1960s place these people in precarious situations. Often they were employed to comply with affirmative action guidelines, and their positions are without power. They are reluctant to employ too many blacks for fear of criticism. A black superintendent of prisons in a large city, who was probably appointed to the post

108

because of the high percentage of black prisoners, explains his dilemma: "If I hire two people, one better be black and one better be white. If I hire two blacks, people will say, 'Aha, I know what he's up to,' and if I hire two whites, I'll be called an Uncle Tom."[29]

A black physician in Mississippi was refused permission to practice in a hospital. "In the fall of 1977, I began private practice in Canton [Mississippi] and applied for medical staff privileges at Madison General. Even though I am the only private physician here who has been certified by the American Board of Family Practice, and even though my references are laudatory, the hospital denied my application without even an interview."[30]

In some respects middle-class blacks are more likely to encounter racism than their poor fellow blacks in the slums, for the poor blacks are likely to be shielded from white people. Hence, they are spared the subtle discrimination encountered by members of the middle class in employment and public accommodations. One might not know if one is passed over for promotion because of race or some other factor, but given the nature of American society, it is not unreasonable to first assume that race was the deciding factor.

THE BLACK MIDDLE CLASS AND SOCIAL RESPONSIBILITY

There is widespread feeling among black people that those who have achieved middle-class status are more concerned with preserving their positions than they are about the plight of the vast majority of other blacks who are poor. As early as the 1950s E. Franklin Frazier wrote, "The black bourgeoisie have shown no interest in the 'liberation' of Negroes except as it affected their own status or acceptance by the white community."[31] It was Frazier's view that "the masses regard the black bourgeoisie as simply those who have been 'lucky in getting money' which enables them to engage in conspicuous consumption." He felt that "the black bourgeoisie has exploited the Negro masses as ruthlessly as have whites."[32]

During the civil rights movement class differences tended to play a less important function in the black community than the drive for liberation. Physicians, school teachers, businessmen and women, judges, attorneys, social workers, and others joined the lines of march with welfare recipients and factory and domestic workers in an effort to eradicate segregation and discrimination based on race. At the height of the civil rights movement many prominent blacks pledged (and contributed) their support to black leaders who were considered to be controversial. Such support varied anywhere from an offer to post bail for a well-known Communist arrested on the unsupported charge of murder, to participation in local demonstrations against segregation. For a few years it appeared that the black community had achieved a significant degree of unity that cut across class lines.[33] This is not to imply that all middle-class blacks have abandoned the struggle of the black masses. Dedicated middle-class blacks may still be found in the forefront of the struggle for greater black freedom. And, of course, middle-class blacks continue to support the major civil rights organizations: the National Association for the Advancement of Colored People, the National Urban League, People United to Serve Humanity, and the Southern Christian Leadership Conference.

In recent years, however, Americans have become known as the "me" generation, meaning that many are largely self-centered and absorbed in egotistical pursuits. Just as such a characterization is no doubt inappropriate for all Americans, it is so pervasive as to be applicable to the society as a whole. And, from all accounts this is as characteristic of the black middle class as of other Americans. According to one observer, the black middle class "is drifting more and more distant from its less fortunate brothers."[34] The director of a community organization in Chicago said: "For years we paid pitifully little attention to classism. We didn't think blacks would really fall prey to it, but now we've come to recognize it as being a problem, and one as venal as racism."[35] Although this assessment is an exaggeration, it indicates what some local black leaders are thinking.

An article in the *Wall Street Journal* reports that "relations between middle-class and lower-class blacks sometimes become strained, those who are trapped in the slums may resent and distrust blacks whose careers are thriving." For example, one lawyer reports that she is often referred to as a "house nigger" because she attended private schools and the Episcopal church. "It's your own rejecting you," she said, "and it hurts."[36] Although this lawyer may be hurt, there is growing evidence that many are not. For example, many middle-class blacks have put forth efforts to block low-income housing developments in their neighborhoods. And often they have joined forces with middle-class whites in these endeavors.

On the tenth anniversary of the release of the *Report of the National Advisory Commission on Civil Disorders,* published after rebellions of the mid-1960s, the *New York Times* published a series of articles on the black community a decade later. One of these articles concerned relations between middle-class and poor blacks. Its thrust was that although the commission had predicted the impending development of distinct societies for blacks and whites, it had not predicted the development of two societies for the black community, one consisting of the middle class and the other of poor blacks. It maintains that the tension between these two classes is not unlike that the commission found between blacks and whites and that there is a possibility of class violence in the black community. It is reported that "low-income blacks feel that their protests and rioting made possible the gains by the middle class, which is now running from ghetto areas to 'live white.' Some experts, as well as members of the middle class, acknowledged that their lifestyle was closer to that of the white middle class than to that of poor blacks."[37] One cannot deny that little racial progress has been made without protest, and the protests since 1965 have been conducted mainly through the efforts of poor blacks in central city slums. Many a middle-class black person owes his or her education and subsequent employment to these protests. Indeed, some of the middle-class blacks today were themselves participants in those struggles.

When asked in an interview, "Are the black poor hostile to the black middle class?" the director of the National Association of Minority Contractors replied: "That's more of a figment of the media's invention. If I were termed to be in the black middle-class, I could walk in the same place with a black that is on the lower end of the totem pole and be faced with the same racism." He continued, "You get the most animosity [toward] a black who has been elected or appointed to a position that could help lower-class blacks and who has not done it. Take a black alderman or black councilman who remains, you know, a handkerchief-head lackey. He will get the scorn of those who think government services could help them."[38]

A different view was provided by a black physician in Chicago: "Middle-class blacks have by and large forgotten their roots, and this is the most heinous crime of all. They can have a tremendous impact on the national scene, political and otherwise. We have the potential to force change, and we are wasting that potential."[39]

There is no doubt some friction between the very poor blacks and those who have achieved middle-class status, but the discord has been magnified by recent writers on the subject. Where there are sharp class differences, conflict is inevitable. But are the differences between any two segments of the black population so great, and the segments so large, as to make for class warfare in the black community, as has been suggested? No one can minimize the plight of blacks who have rarely, if ever, been part of the labor force. Nor is it impossible to understand their anger and frustration, but the very poor blacks understand that the American economic system and the society's racism are responsible for their plight, not middle-class blacks. So when black people in New York virtually destroy the third largest black-owned business in the United States during a power failure, this is not necessarily antiblack. Rather it is a response to the dismal economic position in which they find themselves.

A recent article on the "black elite" in *U.S. News and World Report* details the various ways in which wealthy blacks are providing assistance to those remaining in the slums.[40] Some lawyers, doctors, teachers, and other professionals are simply not in a position to employ large numbers of blacks, and what assistance they can provide must be reserved for members of their immediate and extended families. Middle-class blacks sponsor fund-raising events for black education, civil rights, and community organizations. In Philadelphia a group of black professionals and others sponsor a project that permits poor youth to spend time in the workplaces of those who are successful. A black fraternity supports training programs and provides financial assistance for college students. And a major black publishing company sponsors a series of fashion shows in nearly 100 cities with the proceeds going to local charities. Vernon Jordan, former president of the National Urban League, takes the position that "the black middle class is still very much involved in the struggles and heartbreaks of Black America. It must be remembered that it is their sisters, brothers, cousins, aunts, uncles and friends who are the victims of America's failure to deal with her greatest domestic problem." He cites a 1978 survey of 2,000 successful blacks (more than one-half earned at least $35,000 yearly) that demonstrated that "far from being isolated from the mass of Black America, the black middle class is an integral part of it." Some 90 percent indicated that they felt a great sense of black pride; 87 percent felt that they had a responsibility to the black community as a whole; and 75 percent supported the civil rights movement.[41]

In this chapter we have attempted to review various definitions of what middle-class status means in the black community. Those who write on the subject use a variety of indicators, usually occupation or income. And almost all use some income figure to delineate the black middle-class population. These figures differ greatly, but it appears that most would agree that a minimum annual salary of $15,000 would constitute middle-class status. As for occupation, some writers have employed categories clearly not middle class. Many agree, however, that white-collar occupations are fairly well correlated with other indicators of middle-class status.

The contemporary black middle class is probably more like the white middle class in its lifestyle than it is like poor blacks. Unlike the black middle class of several decades ago, its members are less segregated; hence, they have a chance to observe middle-class whites and emulate their lifestyles.

Unlike previous generations of the black middle class, the present generation is likely to have fewer problems of race. The society is much more open now than in the past. However, blacks in the middle class continue to face problems of discrimination in housing and employment. And, for many, their positions are precarious because they are employed in posts easily abolished during periods of austerity. The present administration in Washington is cutting back in areas where many of them are employed.

The black middle class is becoming increasingly isolated from poor blacks; they, like white Americans, have become more individualistic and self-centered. Although many (perhaps most) are the first in their families to attain middle-class status, and some of them achieved their positions as a result of the struggles waged by the black masses, they often forget their origins. For example, in a survey in 1978 conducted in the urban North, respondents were asked, "Do you think disturbances, such as those in Detroit and Newark in 1967, helped or hurt the cause of black rights?" One-fourth of those whites polled responded that they had helped the cause, and 35 percent of blacks gave a similar response. In both cases, a minority felt that these events had hurt the cause, while about one-third of both groups said they felt that they had made no difference.[42] Despite the strain in relations, there seems to be little evidence to support the often-repeated notion that the strife between classes in the black community borders on class warfare.

VII

AND THE BLACK UNDERCLASS

JUST as there has been some increase in the percentage of blacks in the middle class in the past few years, there has been a startling growth of the black underclass. This development is serious because it means that these black youths are in the society but not a part of it. There is some doubt that these people will ever find their way into the mainstream of the larger society. They are usually ignored until frustration and anger drive them to rebel against a society that has cast them aside, as was the case with the urban rebellions of the 1960s. Then political leaders rush to establish makeshift work programs for a few months before they again forget about the plight of the black underclass. They have no institutional ties and no advocates.

In the 1960s the black middle class could be expected to champion the cause of civil rights, including those of the black underclass. But today the black middle class appears to be primarily concerned with self-advancement and maintaining its precarious status.

DEFINING THE BLACK UNDERCLASS

Perhaps the most salient characteristic of the black underclass is its poverty. It is difficult to know how many people are involved because statistics on unemployment are notoriously inadequate. One source estimates that there were approximately 381,000 unemployed black teenagers in 1978.[1] Some federal agencies have attempted to give some idea of the number of young people who find themselves in this vicious set of circumstances. The Bureau of Labor Statistics usually categorizes them into teenagers (ages sixteen to nineteen) and older youths (ages twenty to twenty-four). The teenagers receive the greatest attention in the literature because they sustain significantly higher rates of unemployment. Since the end of World War II their plight has continued to deteriorate.

The striking thing about teenage unemployment is that white youths fare much better in securing employment than do blacks. Throughout the decade of the 1970s, for example, the rate for blacks remained more than twice as high as that of whites (Table 7.1). These unemployment rates for black teenagers no doubt represent an underenumeration, for most of them live in the central sections of large cities where little is known about the inhabitants, including their numbers. And these data are disputed by many writers. For example, the *New York Times* estimates the number of jobless black teenagers at 400,000 at any time, and one economist feels that another 700,000 "have disappeared from the system." They are "not unemployed, not employed, not in school – they are on the streets."[2]

Vernon Jordan estimates the unemployment rate for black teenagers at 50 percent or more.[3] And in an editorial, the *New York Times* puts the figure at "perhaps more than 60 percent."[4]

Clearly the underclass includes males and females of all ages, but emphasis has been placed on youth unemployment, usually that of males, no doubt because these people are capable of massive destruction resulting from their frustrations, and this is the population among whom the crime rate is highest. Many teenage members of the underclass are from

Table 7.1. *Unemployment rate for teenagers (ages 16–19) by race, selected years, 1970–79*

	1970	1973	1975	1977	1978	1979
Black	29.1	30.2	36.9	38.3	36.3	33.5
White	13.5	12.6	17.9	15.4	13.9	13.9

Source: George Iden, "The Labor Force Experience of Black Youth: A Review," *Monthly Labor Review*, August 1980.

families who are themselves members of the underclass. But most of the emphasis here will be placed on teenagers and young adults. They are, after all, citizens who might otherwise be considered future leaders. Rather, what we have is a group of citizens who have been left behind by the larger society. Federal, state, and local governments have made modest attempts to stem the tide of the growth of the underclass, but for a variety of reasons that will be discussed, their numbers increase rather than decrease.

Perhaps two of the major defining characteristics of the black underclass are their poverty and the social decay in which they are forced to survive. According to Douglas Glasgow, they constitute "a significantly younger population than the poor of previous generations[;] these young Blacks, some as young as thirteen or fourteen, are already earmarked for failure – they are often undereducated, jobless, without salable skills or the social credentials to gain access to mainstream life. They are rendered obsolete before they can even begin to pursue a meaningful role in society."[5] There is little doubt that if these persons were white, considerably greater efforts would be made to ameliorate their plight. White youth unemployment, far above the national average, is only about one-third the black rate.

Many persons are of the opinion that these youths are incapable of learning, but in interviews one finds them to be highly intelligent and knowledgeable of the world around them. Most are eager for meaningful employment, but because of societal factors they have been abandoned to a life of hopelessness. Often they are forced to engage in criminal activities, a rational response to the circumstances in which they find themselves. And it must be noted that since these people are treated as animals, they frequently respond in kind.

Much has been written about the growing division in the black community between members of the underclass and the middle class, but most of the evidence indicates that the anger and hostility are directed at the larger society rather than at other blacks. They know that although some members of the middle class remain aloof from their plight, it is the societal institutions, controlled by whites, that are responsible for their condition. When they rebel, as is often the case, they strike at the most convenient targets, knowing that if they take their protests downtown they will simply be slaughtered.

In a rich nation, willing to spend hundreds of billions of dollars for war, it is nothing short of criminal that employment cannot be provided for these few hundred thousand youths. In listening to their conversations one is keenly aware that they know government officials are responsible for their destitution. The schools share the blame, but simply because the schools are failing to educate them is no reason for the government's apathy.

Most of the underclass youth have few organizational ties, aside from those with members of their families and friends. In the communities in which they are forced to survive there are few social organizations to provide the necessary support. Most are not eligible for welfare because they are male and young, and few other programs provide any support. Generally, they are forced to rely on the surplus commodities and food stamp programs of the Department of Agriculture.

PERMANENT UNEMPLOYMENT

That members of the underclass have little formal education, no employment, and few job skills is a serious indictment of the larger society. It is difficult enough to be black in the United States and when this is combined with these factors, there appears to be little hope for these outcasts. There have been some attempts by the federal government to reach these citizens, but rather than declining, their numbers are increasing. And given the Reagan administration's proposed budget reductions for social and economic programs, one can only suspect that when the situation really becomes intolerable, there will be rebellions throughout the country. The members of the underclass have demonstrated on several occasions that they are capable of massive property destruction and of fighting a guerrilla war with the police for days.

There is a widespread myth in the United States that those citizens do not want work, that they prefer to live off government handouts. Most research studies have demonstrated that this impression is in error. Public opinion polls have repeatedly shown that the jobless are eager to work. For example, a recent poll showed that 75 percent of the unemployed would accept jobs viewed as menial, even those jobs paying salaries below the minimum wage.[6] The members of the underclass invariably report that they would rather work than experience the degradation that characterizes their lives. And in Atlanta one federal job was advertised, but the crush of people anxious to work was so great that the crowd broke through a plate glass window to get into the line. Such incidents have been repeated around the country on many occasions.

A young man on the streets of Harlem expressed his desire for work: "I ain't no dummy. If I just had a little jive job, I'd be all right." He continued, "It ain't that I ain't got enough here to occupy my mind – I honest to truly do. But it ain't the kind of stuff I want my mind on."[7] This young man said he had been sent to a job by an employment agency, only to find that when he knocked on the door he was told that the nursing home had been closed for several years. He became disillusioned and never returned to the agency.

One young man from Watts (Los Angeles) blamed racism for his unemployment: "I messed up some. I can't take it away, because I did it. But I know it's harder for me out there just try to get the job you want. White boys get the chance first." Still another: "Even if you had training and know how to do the job, once you show up and ask for the machine operating job, and the man sees you, he wants to give you a broom and start you sweeping. Well, I'd rather not work than sweep no floor."[8]

Discrimination no doubt plays a major role in maintaining the black underclass, as these cases indicate. But other factors have contributed to a situation in which black youths and young adults have experienced increasing unemployment rates since World War II. Although the current rate is difficult to pinpoint, it exceeds by far the national rate during the depression. An analyst for the Congressional Budget Office reports that black youths were affected disproportionately by the unfavorable job market of the 1970s.[9] In addition, he reports that black students experience difficulty finding part-time jobs. Both of these reasons for the high unemployment of black teenagers indicate that, among other things, race plays a crucial role in their high unemployment rates.

It is sometimes maintained that in addition to discrimination, black youths suffer high unemployment rates because in the last several decades factories and other prospective places of employment have moved from the central cities to the suburbs along with the middle class. Entry-level jobs in such places make it impossible for young blacks to seek employment. As one St. Louis youth pointed out in an interview, "I've been to the employment office and they've got jobs there only in the suburbs and I don't have a car. It wouldn't be worth my time to pay bus fare, taxes, lunch and stuff for a job way out in the suburbs that pays $2.65 an hour."[10] Many business enterprises have relocated from the central city to the suburbs for a variety of reasons, not the least of which is crime.

Jobs that had traditionally been reserved for blacks – waiters, bellmen, kitchen helpers in restaurants, farm workers, and messengers – have, in the past few decades, gone to the influx of undocumented workers entering the country. Many of these persons – Latin Americans and Asians – have entered the country illegally and are willing to work for wages below the minimum. Estimates on the number of undocumented workers vary anywhere from four to twelve million. Unscrupulous businessmen frequently take advantage of these undocumented workers and pay them as little as one dollar per hour. No one should be expected to work for such wages, no matter how destitute.

Large numbers of black youth have had encounters with the police, and arrest records (for real or imagined crimes) complicate the employment picture. In New Orleans, for example, a young black man had been arrested seven times. Because of this record he feared being arrested if he should seek employment. "If I so much as walk into some of those downtown stores," seeking a job, he feared being arrested again. He constantly walked the streets hoping someone would need "a man to load or unload a truck or something."[11]

In the past few years white women have entered the labor market in large numbers. According to the Bureau of Labor Statistics, the work force increased by three million in one year. Of this number approximately 1.5 million were white women.[12] This factor accounts for some unemployment among black youths. Frequently, white females are better educated and trained than black youths, many of whom have dropped out of school with few skills. With a limited number of jobs available, they can hardly expect to secure them.

The Bureau of Labor Statistics gives additional reasons for high black teenage unemployment.[13] It is claimed that the post–World War II baby boom crowded the labor market throughout the 1960s and 1970s. This rapid population growth, it is said, resulted in an excess supply of younger workers, making employment difficult. But it must also be added that since the white teenage employment rate has remained relatively steady during this period, again discrimination plays a major role in teenage black unemployment.

Still another factor cited by the Bureau of Labor Statistics for the high unemployment among black teenagers is that they have been "priced out" of the labor force by the minimum wage. The argument goes that if employers are forced to pay the minimum wage to these young workers, they are likely to substitute older, more productive workers. This effectively restricts the opportunities of younger workers, but white teenage employment, again, has remained fairly stable for several decades, while that of blacks has steadily decreased.

Because of these and other factors, many of the government-sponsored programs designed to assist black youth have had little, if any, effect on the problem of black youth unemployment. The *Wall Street Journal* conducted a study of black youth unemployment in Dade County, Florida, in 1979.[14] Two youth job training centers were compared. One, in a black neighborhood, where all the trainees were black and from poor families, had experienced cuts in its federal funding, causing dissatisfaction among the staff and the young people. Another center, serving a largely white population, where at least one parent held a full-time job, had its support increased at about the same time.

For nearly three decades now the federal government has been appropriating funds for programs intended to curb black teenage joblessness, but each year the unemployment rate increases. Over a period of ten years some $40 billion was spent with little to show for the money. In 1978 alone some $12 billion was spent on such programs. In addition to government spending, private businesses established their own programs to curb the unemployment rate. But by far the biggest programs were those in which the government became the employer of the hard-core unemployed. Many of these programs were established by the Comprehensive Employment and Training Act (CETA), which established job-training programs in public service and private industry. CETA has been funded at a rate of approximately $11 billion annually, providing jobs for hundreds of thousands of hard-core unemployed youth. In addition, the Youth Employment and Demonstrations Project of 1977 and the Department of Labor's Office of Youth Programs have provided millions of dollars for employment and training, again to public and private agencies.

There is some feeling that such programs have failed because of corruption, inability to adequately serve the targeted population, and because the youth are poorly motivated.[15] The public schools must bear the lion's share of the responsibility, for it is nothing short of disgraceful that hundreds of thousands of functionally illiterate teenagers are graduated from high school each year. Still others drop out of school for lack of motivation. In a world becoming more complex, they are destined for permanent unemployment. It is commonly thought that lack of motivation is one of the major factors contributing to teenage unemployment. Yet little, if anything, is being done to cope with this massive problem, either by the schools or the training programs.

There can be little argument with Kenneth Clark that the black underclass is a function of American racial oppression.[16] He maintains that although many blacks benefited from the Civil Rights Act of 1964, the masses (especially in the North) remained trapped in slums without employment and with poor educational facilities. They were ignored by the society. One can only wonder what would happen if the teenage unemployment rate for whites approached that of blacks. There is every reason to believe that a national effort would be launched to eradicate the problem. Given such resources and concern, the manmade problem of the black underclass could also be solved.

The outlook for government funding of programs to assist

the chronically unemployed young is grim. The Carter administration allocated some $247 million for 225 youth programs around the country.[17] These projects ranged anywhere from help to single teenage parents to agricultural entrepreneurship programs. Twelve percent of the money, more than $30 million, was allocated to minorities. The present administration has not only decreased the total amount of the projects, but it has reduced the minority allocation to 6 percent. Many of the minority programs in operation when the Reagan administration took office have been eliminated, including some of the programs for which agencies had been assured funding. Such a situation has led many observers to describe the Reagan administration as racist in its approach to youth employment programs.

LIFESTYLE

The members of the black underclass, especially those males between sixteen and nineteen years of age, have carved out for themselves a lifestyle geared toward minimizing the hopelessness and despair that is so characteristic of their existence. Work being an important part of one's self-esteem, measures must be taken to sustain their self-esteem since they are unemployed. In far too many cases their parents before them have been unemployed for long periods so that they have very few positive images with which to identify. Unlike their counterparts who have remained in school or who have entered college, their associations tend to be with fellow members of the underclass, and their lives revolve around the streets, where they frequently become involved in illegal activities.

A recently published study of the black underclass in the Watts section of Los Angeles details life on the street for these social rejects.[18] These people were all considered to be failures because they were not in school; they were denied employment, and had no prospects for future employment. Some of them accepted the label applied to them and simply adapted to life on the street. Some were steady drug users and drank cheap wine. In order to secure money they engaged in minor hustling and begging.

Others have held out in the hope of eventually securing

menial employment. They expect to receive a chance to prove their capabilities in mainstream society. Still others have adapted by simply manipulating the environment in which they find themselves to maximize their potential. They felt that they could prove themselves if given a chance, but these hopes soon led to despair, and they concentrated on survival. This meant hustling in the streets.

The street culture of the underclass is largely an urban phenomenon. Some of the members have migrated from rural areas, and they land on the dreary streets of urban areas, streets with vacant lots, bars, liquor stores, pawnshops, and movie houses. In many cases they select special places to spend their time together. Often it is a vacant lot or simply on the street corner. In Watts it is the parking lot. And the parking lot culture is often both dull and turbulent, frequently requiring keen intelligence. The most enterprising in the group are frequently well dressed and own automobiles, although they do not hold legitimate jobs. Because the people are intelligent and articulate, they frequently serve as role models for the other members of the underclass.

According to Douglas Glasgow, another category of the underclass is what he calls the "activist," one "who obtains money through acts of vandalism, robbery, and theft. Within this category, there is a breakdown into 'strong arm studs,' 'stealers,' and those who 'rip off.'"[19] The strong armers secure money through acts of burglary, frequently with the use of weapons. They concentrate on stores and banks for money. The stealers secure money by selling and exchanging stolen goods. Unlike the strong armers, the stealers prey on the local community, stealing household appliances, clothing, and furniture. The rip-off hustler operates spontaneously, stealing whatever he can from whatever source.

The underclass men maintain female companions, but they are unable to occupy the role of breadwinner in the relationship. The underclass black woman is able to generate more income than the man; more low-paying jobs are available to her, and it is easier for her to receive welfare. In addition, they sometimes engage in prostitution. Consequently, the woman often provides money for her companion. In return the male serves as her protector and acts as a surrogate father, if there are children. He is, in short, the man around the house.

As is true of the larger society, drugs are widespread among the underclass. But these are rarely hard drugs, and they serve to cushion a marginal and difficult existence. But contrary to popular opinion, most of the men do not use hard drugs, for they are expensive and are controlled by sources outside the slums. The major drug used by these men is marijuana, largely because it is relatively inexpensive (depending on quantity) and readily available. Such men can be seen in their hangouts hawking individual marijuana cigarettes (joints), but rarely do they sell marijuana in larger quantities.

It is likely that if a black male lives in a large city, and does not attend college, he will encounter the criminal justice system by the age of 25. His first encounter is likely to be with the police, and because of police contempt for the underclass this experience will shape his attitudes toward the criminal justice system. The police are almost uniformly hated, viewed as the army of occupation in the black community. The police stop, question, and arrest members of the underclass, making their very existence a crime. No other category of citizens is treated with such arbitrariness. It is no wonder that the police are so hated. Black males who venture from their neighborhoods are routinely stopped and questioned, and within the neighborhood black males are made to feel impotent in the face of arbitrary authority. For reasons that would never obtain in white neighborhoods, black people are arrested, beaten, and thrown in jail. This contributes to the lack of mobility among the underclass; with all the other factors working against their becoming productive members of society, it is doubly difficult to secure employment with a police record. And a significant proportion of the underclass has such records.

Many of the black underclass youth have dropped out of high school before graduation. They are bored with school and are not motivated by their teachers. In Miami one such dropout explained: The teachers are "so bad I fall asleep all the time." When they drop out of school they frequently sell marijuana, engage in robbery, pickpocketing, burglary, breaking and entering, mugging, and the numbers racket. But there is every reason to believe that they would prefer working, if given a chance. They are aware that they are members of an underclass whose prospects for permanent employment are grim. Consequently, they engage in crime "to stay alive."

And the black underclass

Although a significant number of high school dropouts are functionally illiterate (the *New York Times* estimates that 42 percent of black seventeen year olds are functionally illiterate[20]) many are quite intelligent. According to Douglas Glasgow: "He is highly articulate, bright, and conceptually oriented."[21] And, "Survival as an underclass person is an excruciatingly painful social existence that requires herculean individual effort, guile, wit, and much perseverance."[22]

According to one writer, the underclass in the black community is synonymous with the lower-lower class. He sees them as "folk" blacks who "rank lowest in income, occupational skills, employment, education, family stability, and the acquisition of status symbols." Furthermore, "Abject resignation to unsufferable conditions permeates lives compounded by a persistently nagging sense of despair, hopelessness, and frustration."[23] These are among the most unfortunate citizens of the United States, members of the society but not really a part of it.

PERSONAL RELATIONS AND COPING

There have been several studies of the black underclass, and if one visits the proper section of almost any sizable American city, they may be seen, usually standing on street corners. As is the case in developing nations with high unemployment, these men (and sometimes women) are usually there all day, every day, while most other members of the society are working. These people are not working and few, in government or out, appear to be concerned about their plight. They are poorly educated and possess few skills. But this is not to imply that they are incapable of acquiring the necessary skills for meaningful employment. Furthermore, they are not unlike other citizens in their personal relations and in their struggle for survival. What they often lack is a sense of self-esteem, a result of having been brutalized by the larger society.

Hanging out on the corner in Washington

Elliot Liebow, an anthropologist, studied street corner men in Washington, D.C., in the early 1960s.[24] The details of the lives of two dozen men who shared a street corner were recorded. When they worked it was at low-status occupations: day laborers, menial workers in retail or service trades, and unskilled construction workers. Most were unemployed for long periods. Some of the men were married, others single; some lived with their wives; others lived with women who were not their wives.

These men spent their time on a corner in downtown Washington, near the New Deal Carry-out Shop, and within walking distance from the White House and the Smithsonian Institution. In the block were a liquor store, a dry cleaning shop, and a shoe repair shop. The neighborhood was known as one with problems – crime, poverty, child neglect, and the highest rate of public assistance in the city.

Although most of the men were in their twenties and had attended high school, many were functionally illiterate. The greatest concern of these men was employment. As a means of maintaining their self-esteem some of them worked at night cleaning offices, removing garbage, mopping floors, and cleaning toilets. Their take-home pay made them among the poorest-paid employees and explains the high rate of turnover. For many who saw them on the corner daily the feeling was that they did not want to work, but there were few jobs in the neighborhood and many of the nonunion jobs were twenty to twenty-five miles away in the Maryland suburbs.

Many of the men had wives and children to support, but they were unable to secure jobs to support their families. Furthermore, on some low-paying jobs it was assumed that the men would steal from their employer, and the wages were scaled down. It should be emphasized, as Liebow points out, that "*the street corner man puts no lower value on the job than does the larger society around him.*"[25] The problem is that the street corner men were relegated to the lowest-level jobs in the society. The work was hard and dirty and was at the bottom of the prestige ladder. The members of the larger society have a low opinion of such jobs. The same is true of the street corner man.

For the street corner men, their lives have been a series of failures. In many cases they came from homes where their fathers left the family because they could not cope with the loss of self-esteem associated with the inability to support the family. As Liebow described the situation: "Armed with models who have failed, convinced of his own worthlessness, illiterate and unskilled, he enters marriage and the job market with the smell of failure all around him. Jobs are only intermittently available. They are almost always menial, sometimes hard, and never pay enough to support a family."[26]

Few of the street corner men maintained stable relationships with their wives or lovers. In some cases children were born out of casual, short-term unions. And only in a minority of cases did the men live with the women who were the mothers of their children. Some men had children in the cities and towns from which they migrated. In almost all cases, the children of such unions are reared by their mothers. In some cases these children were reared by the father's mother. One of the major reasons most of these men rejected marriage is that they are confronted with their failure daily. True manliness (especially the ability to provide for one's family) remained an illusion.

Personal relationships are important to the men on the corner. Each man establishes close personal ties with other men. There are, of course, cliques or closely knit networks of friendship. These are the people he turns to in emergencies and other times of crisis. He gives them goods and services, which are reciprocated. These relationships are maintained on the corner, for these men have few friends elsewhere. Informal kinship arrangements are widespread. In some cases they share the same room and may be referred to as "brothers" or "cousins." Clothes and other personal possessions are shared.

The inability of the street corner men to retain employment, and the ever-present prospect of failure, drive them to seek out others like themselves on the street corner. For it is the way in which one makes a living and the kind of living one makes that bestow self-esteem in American society.

Abandoned in Harlem

Unlike the underclass in Watts or the street corner men in Washington, there is a group of young blacks in Harlem who have all the characteristics of the underclass, but their situation is somewhat unique. Claude Brown has written about them in *The Children of Ham.*[27] These (male and female) youth range in age from fourteen to twenty-two and live collectively in apartments in an abandoned building owned by the city of New York. There is no hot water or electricity in the apartments, and the building is infested with rats the size of cats. In some of the apartments garbage is piled five or six feet high. Drug addicts frequent the other apartments, utilizing them as "shooting galleries."

In the building there are holes in the walls large enough for people to walk from one apartment to another. The Children of Ham (or Hamites) occupy three apartments, each containing two or three bedrooms. They sleep on cots or mattresses scavenged from the street. They do little cooking, aside from making sandwiches. They take pride in these apartments, for most of them came from homes torn by conflict and heroin use. In many cases both parents were junkies. There is no rigid division of labor, but somehow different people end up doing appropriate work in order to make the experiment work. To demonstrate their appreciation, they have put curtains and even shades in the apartments and have covered the ceilings with multicolored tinfoil.

These people, largely teenagers, have refused to succumb to heroin, although most of them have been around it most of their lives, either at home or in the neighborhood. They drink whiskey and wine, and smoke marijuana. Those who are in school appear to enjoy it and attend regularly. Although they are all from underclass families, they have strong desires to advance themselves by completing high school, and some have even indicated a desire to attend college. Perhaps the thing that keeps these unfortunate youths together is the need for companionship and friendship, which they did not find at home.

A few words about some of the Hamites. A fifteen-year-old seventh grader whom some considered to be mentally retarded because he stuttered eagerly took up residence with the Hamites. He had been waiting for many years to leave home and gave this as his major motivation: He went into his mother's room where she was praying for his brother who was seriously ill with pneumonia. He heard her pray that if one of her children should die, it should not be his ill brother but him instead. She said, among other things, that he was crippled and would not have a very good life. Shortly after he moved in with the Hamites he stopped stuttering. In addition to being the interior decorator for the apartment, he developed into a craftsman, repairing broken things; he also raised pigeons on the roof. Like many other teenagers in New York City, he always managed to have an aerosol spray can that he used to paint his nickname, "Salt-Nobody," whenever he could.

An excellent gardener, he planted marijuana for the group. But his main position was keeping things working. He earned money for the group by making scooters out of two-by-fours and one roller skate. These he sold for two dollars apiece. The members of the group considered him to be a person like everyone else, one with some value. He became more outgoing, and just as he profited from the arrangement, so did the others.

An eighteen-year-old young woman joined the Children of Ham. She became both big sister and mother to the group. Her mother died when she was eleven, and she had been on her own since then. She had been a junkie and had been to jail and to reform school. In addition, she had been a prostitute and a drug dealer. The eighth child from a family of ten children (with five different fathers), she never knew her father. The Hamites are the closest thing she had ever had to a family, and she was grateful to be accepted by the group. When asked about her mother's death she said that since her mother was on welfare she did not think there was a funeral. But she was not sure.

Having lived on the streets longer than any of the other Hamites, she has suffered greatly at the hands of the men she knew and the police. She tells stories of heroin overdoses and police brutality. In spite of all this she is considered to be one of the more compassionate Hamites.

Although the Hamites do not have a leader, the person most often listened to is a bright sixteen-year-old boy. On the streets most of his life, he left home because his mother was a heroin addict. One day the neighbor across the hall called to tell him and his siblings that their mother was ill. But what had happened was that she had been arrested for shoplifting and was in jail. When she returned from jail her first act was not to see about the children, who had been staying with a neighbor; rather, she shot more heroin. At this point the young man left for the streets. He says he is determined to find a good job and take his younger brothers and sisters to live with him.

This young man is a strong black nationalist, and like so many others, he feels nothing but contempt for the police. About the New York City police he had this to say: "Cops are some of the foulest forms of life out there. You see them askin' to be killed all the time with those stupid acts, all the silly changes they take people through. They go around begging to be killed. That ol' racist white police department down there, they send those stupid young white cowboys full of racism to black neighborhoods, you know, and let 'em raise hell. Then they act surprised when somebody ices one of 'em. That's because whitey thinks blacks supposed to keep on goin' for it."[28]

The Children of Ham are not the conventional underclass. In some regards they are even worse, if that is possible. Little is known about such youth, but in New York City alone thousands of poor children live in much the same manner. If one rides the subway late at night or early morning, one can see many children there who have no place to live and who have been abandoned by their families. Having been treated as animals all their lives, it is no wonder that they grow up incapable of living in organized society.

As Claude Brown has written, "The common tragedy among these youngsters is that by the time they reach the age of nineteen or twenty they are thoroughly and irreversibly demoralized. All the ambition and drive they once had is permanently crushed out of them."[29]

RACE AND YOUTH UNEMPLOYMENT

For more than a decade the transition of youth from the family and school to a productive adulthood has been a major concern of government and community organizations. The greatest impediments to making a smooth transition in a complex labor market continue to fall on minority youth. The point has

131

been made here that the problems of youth unemployment are essentially racial in nature. And it should be pointed out that although most members of the underclass are part of the mass of youth unemployment, not all teenagers without jobs are part of the underclass.

There are notable differences in the unemployment problems of black and white youth by sex. In 1955 the unemployment rate for black males sixteen to nineteen years of age was 13.4 percent and 12.4 percent for those twenty to twenty-four years old. Comparable rates for white males were 11.3 percent and 7 percent, respectively. By 1978 the unemployment rate for white males sixteen to nineteen was only 13.5 percent and for those twenty to twenty-four it was 7.6 percent. In contrast, the unemployment rate for black males had almost tripled in both age groups. For black males sixteen to nineteen the unemployment rate reached 38.4 percent, and it reached 21.4 percent for the twenty to twenty-four-year-old group.

The situation for young black females also worsened in relationship to white males and females. In the period 1955 to 1978 the unemployment rate for black females sixteen to nineteen years of age doubled from 19.2 to 38.4 percent, and for those twenty to twenty-four years of age from 13 percent to 21.3 percent. By contrast, the unemployment rates for the first category of white female youth only increased from 9.1 percent to 14.4 percent, and for women in the second group unemployment rose only from 5.1 to 8.3 percent for the period 1955 to 1978.

The historical discrimination against black youth was institutionalized by the end of the 1970s. Fewer than one-half (47.2 percent) of the black male teenagers sixteen to nineteen had work experience in 1978, compared to nearly three-fourths of white males in the same age group, and although 93.2 percent of white males twenty to twenty-four had some work experience, only about three-fourths of black males had work experience. White male youth, similar to adult white males, maintained their hegemony on obtaining jobs and work experience. The recessions did not significantly harm the opportunities for labor market participation by white male youths, and white males twenty to twenty-four were a major exception to the pattern of youths working in jobs with little training, as they often found jobs with small employers that provided them with technical skills and job contacts for the next step of the job transition to adulthood. Similar to black males, black teenage females were also entering the 1980s with less work experience. Only slightly more than one-third (37.5 percent) of black females sixteen to nineteen had work experience in 1978 compared to almost two-thirds (64.8 percent) of the white females. And, in the ages twenty to twenty-four category, 79 percent of the white females had some work experience compared to approximately two-thirds (63.6 percent) of the black females.

Not only have the rates of unemployment increased for black youth, but their lack of opportunities for *any* work experience during the 1970s placed them in the position where the employers could use this as an excuse for refusing to hire them in the future. Neither history nor the projected labor trend was encouraging.

The labor force participation and employment rates of black youth have declined at a time when their educational attainment has been increasing. Overall, the employment problems of black youth have been best explained by structural factors and discrimination. Structurally serious questions and issues are raised because educational attainment of black youth has not led to employment. In 1977 the clear majority of unemployed black youth had either completed high school or gone to college, whereas only two-fifths were high school dropouts. The educational attainment of unemployed black youth was closer to that of unemployed white youth. Only about 64 percent of the unemployed white youth had at least a high school diploma. It is important to note that educational attainment has not assisted younger blacks in the manner that is generally expected.

Although there is no doubt about the persistence of discrimination, the manner in which it operates in conjunction with other variables is not clear. Black teenage joblessness is affected by a variety of factors. Several factors commonly assumed to be indicators of reasons for black youth joblessness are not usually statistically significant. For example, the residential location of black youth in central cities away from suburban jobs has not been shown to be a major factor affecting the high rate of joblessness among black youth. The minimum wage has had a minimal effect on the reasons for black youth joblessness. And the argument that a reason for high joblessness has been a surplus of black youth in a declining job market is suspect. In addition, data show that among black and white males, the job search methods are not that different, with the exception of the reliance by blacks on state employment services. Thus, the method of seeking work is not a major factor in the inability of black youth to obtain jobs.

The persistence of discrimination in an era of continually unfavorable labor markets does not signal a positive trend for employment among black youth. In this era of potential employment gravity other alternatives must be found.

Retaining young people in school and placing a major emphasis on skills is emerging as a clear alternative to the preoccupation with jobs that are often marginal and offer few learning experiences. A radical perspective is required that recognizes that although schools have historically failed to bolster the skills of youths who found marginal jobs in the secondary labor market, they now have little choice in accepting the role of assisting in the maturation of youth who have almost no chance of finding even the most menial of jobs.

In an editorial that appeared ten years after the *Report of the National Advisory Commission on Civil Disorders*, the *New York Times*, commenting on teenage unemployment, wrote: "Stubborn as the unemployment dilemma may be, the price of failure is too high to be accepted. Alarming numbers of left-out teen-agers turn to crime for survival. But their despair should be even more alarming. No society can call itself civilized when so many of its young are being maimed and destroyed so early in life."[30]

VIII

SOME EDUCATIONAL ISSUES

A MERICA'S black population has always placed a special importance on acquiring formal education. For them it is seen as a means of both social and economic advancement. And although significant gains were made in the 1960s and 1970s, the gap between blacks and whites in educational achievement is still wide, and it affects both income and occupational level. Black people frequently lack access to quality education, thereby relegating them to low occupational status and consequently low incomes. These three variables – education, occupation, and income – are .intertwined in American society, and although some manage to advance themselves on one or two of these, it is usually education that determines one's status in the larger society.

The story of black education in the United States is one where few gains were made in the first decades after the Civil War, to the point where in the 1980s one would almost get the impression that few differences remain in education between the black and white populations. But this notion is a deceptive one as some of the data presented in this chapter will demonstrate. In the first place, secondary education for black children was rigidly segregated (and inferior) prior to the *Brown* decision of 1954. After this decision it was nearly ten years before significant inroads were made in desegregating the nation's schools. Consequently, most of the recent advances have been made in the past fifteen or so years. And there is reason to believe that some of these recent gains have eroded.

The education of black children is in many ways one of the more controversial issues in the society today. Most Americans have rejected the once prevalent notion that black children are incapable of learning, but the view that they are somehow inferior to their white counterparts is still widespread. It is this notion that impels white parents throughout the country to oppose busing. On the postsecondary level the opposition to busing is matched by the resistance to open admissions programs in colleges and universities. After a discussion of the present state of black education, attention will be turned to the two crucial issues of busing and open admissions.

BLACK EDUCATION: PRESENT STATUS

Probably the most basic measure of educational attainment is the number of years of school completed. In 1978, for all persons in the country, 34 percent of adults had not completed high school, whereas the percentage of blacks in the same category was 52.4. Only 3.6 percent of Americans had attained less than five years of school, but among blacks the figure was nearly three times as great – 9.7 percent. Finally, 15.7 percent of all Americans had completed four or more years of college, but only 7.2 percent of blacks were college graduates.[1] These data indicate that the educational gap between blacks and whites is substantial.

It should be noted here that more blacks between the ages of 18 and 24 drop out of high school than enroll in college. In 1967, for example, 35 percent of all blacks in that age category were high school dropouts (compared with 18 percent for whites), and 13 percent were enrolled in college (compared with 27 percent of whites).[2] In 1977 some 24 percent had dropped out and 21 percent were enrolled in college.

Black enrollment in postsecondary education is one of the areas in which greatest advances have been made in recent decades. In 1964 there were 234,000 blacks enrolled in colleges and universities around the country. With the demands for greater educational opportunity brought about by the civil rights movement, the number had increased by 1981 more than four-fold to one million.[3] This respresents an important development for black people, who, throughout their history, have placed so much emphasis on education. It seems that colleges and universities, motivated in part by the black rebellions, were attempting to make some amends for past discrimination.

But the vastly increased number of blacks attending colleges and universities tells only part of the story. Blacks in postsecondary education tend, to a disproportionate extent, to be enrolled in two-year community colleges. In 1979 nearly one-half (46 percent) of all black college students were in the community colleges, whereas about one-third of white students were in the community colleges.[4] Such students are awarded associate degrees, and in many cities and states they are "assured" the right to transfer to a four-year college for the last two years for work toward the baccalaureate degree. But in many cases this is simply not possible, for as those black students receiving associate degrees in 1976 soon learned, only 58 percent of these degrees were creditable toward the baccalaureate. If the community colleges are viewed by black students and their families as the beginning of higher education for themselves and their children, the reality is that they often mean the end of their education and the beginning of marginal occupational careers. And the attrition rates are often disproportionately high.

One researcher characterizes these schools in this manner: "The two-year colleges are process variables designed to cool off society's demand for increased representation in higher education while at the same time insuring continued limited output: earned degrees."[5] As it stands at present, community colleges do not provide egalitarian, low-cost, high-quality education on the postsecondary level.

On the other extreme from community colleges are the universities, the only institutions authorized to offer doctoral degrees. A study conducted by *The Chronicle of Higher Education* reveals that in the years 1973–76 more than 100,000 doctorates were awarded.[6] Nearly nine-tenths of these degrees were awarded to white students, with the vast majority going to white males. Blacks received a total of 3,430 of these degrees, with black males receiving twice as many as black women. Earned doctorates by blacks tend to be concentrated in education, arts and humanities, and social sciences. Few are represented in the sciences and mathematics.

Postsecondary education for black people presents a confusing picture. The impression is conveyed that significant advances have been made, and in some cases this is true. However, it must be tempered with caution for some retrenchment has occurred in some areas. Economic pressures are forcing more and more black students to terminate their formal education with the completion of high school. And while colleges and universities are admitting ever greater numbers, public high schools do not always prepare students for college. For example, in 1970 some 21 percent of black students between fourteen and seventeen years of age who were enrolled in high school were two years below grade level. Only 9 percent of white students were in this category.[7] A significant proportion of these students are likely to drop out before completing high school.

The transporting of school children did not begin with school desegregation. Although it dates back to 1869, busing never became controversial until it was used to achieve equality of educational opportunity through school desegregation. The myths, deliberate distortions, and irrationalities surrounding this emotional issue are legion. Many public officials, from president to local school personnel, have denounced busing, utilizing every possible tactic. Riots have occurred and buses have been burned in an effort to prevent or stall school busing. So vehement have the opponents of busing been, and so persistent in their racial slurs and violence against black children, that many blacks soon learned that "it's not the bus; it's us."

Busing to achieve equality of educational opportunity is of recent origin. The Supreme Court did not rule on the constitutionality of busing to eradicate dual school systems until 1971, when in *Swann v. Charlotte-Mecklenburg Board of Education,* it ruled that school "desegregation plans cannot be limited to the walk-in school," and that busing was an appropriate tool to use in desegregating the Charlotte-Mecklenburg (North Carolina) schools. What the opponents of busing often overlook is that it is required only in those cases where public officials have intentionally segregated the schools along racial lines in violation of the Fourteenth Amendment. At the time of this decision, President Richard Nixon was submitting to Congress "The Student Transportation Moratorium Act of

1972," designed to prevent the Supreme Court and the lower federal courts for a time from enforcing "as they deem necessary, the constitutional right of blacks and other minorities to nonsegregated schools under the 'equal protection' clause of the Fourteenth Amendment."[8]

Busing generates bitter feelings in many Americans. For example, after the *Swann* decision President Nixon, in a nationwide television address, informed the American people that he was opposed to busing children "across a city to an inferior school just to meet some social planner's concept of what is considered to be the correct racial balance." What he failed to tell them was that in the Supreme Court's decision the chief justice explicitly rejected the idea of a "correct racial balance" in favor of a more flexible approach. A black economist who is a strong opponent of busing had this to say on the subject: "It is commonplace to hear of integrated schools where no child of either race dares to enter the toilet alone."[9] The erroneous assumptions here are that the only schools that are integrated are those to which the children are bused, and that in one-race schools there is no violence.

A school administrator in a racially torn Boston school district commented that "busing's got to stack up as the number one error ever made, maybe in the history of mankind. Whoever designed the concept is a lunatic."[10] And a white student in Boston's public schools said: "Nobody's busing me just so some niggers can get a better deal. No one I ever knew had anything to do with it. Niggers don't like their schools, let *them* change 'em, but they don't have the right to tell me what to do."[11]

What is the extent of busing in the United States? And what has been its history? Recent surveys show that over 43 percent of students in the country "ride a school bus every day, and . . . 65 percent take either a school bus or use regular public transportation."[12]

The acceleration of busing came about as a result of public school consolidation, making it possible to replace the one-room school with the consolidated school (Table 8.1). Although the extent of busing pupils is massive, it is very sparingly used for purposes of desegregation. If one reads the accounts of problems schools encounter each September

Some educational issues

Table 8.1. *Growth of school transportation in America*

Year	Number of pupils transported	Total pupils transported (%)
1919–20	356,000	1.7
1921–22	594,000	2.6
1923–24	837,000	3.4
1925–26	1,112,000	4.5
1927–28	1,251,000	5.0
1929–30	1,903,000	7.4
1931–32	2,419,000	9.2
1933–34	2,795,000	10.6
1935–36	3,251,000	12.3
1937–38	3,769,000	14.5
1939–40	4,144,000	16.3
1941–42	4,503,000	18.3
1943–44	4,410,000	19.0
1945–46	5,057,000	21.7
1947–48	5,854,000	24.4
1949–50	6,947,000	27.7
1951–52	7,697,000	29.0
1953–54	8,411,000	32.8
1955–56	9,969,000	35.0
1957–58	10,862,000	36.5
1959–60	12,225,000	37.6
1961–62	13,223,000	38.1
1963–64	14,476,000	38.7
1965–66	15,537,000	39.7
1967–68	17,131,000	42.0
1969–70	18,199,000	43.4

Source: Nicalous Mills (ed.), *The Great School Bus Controversy* (New York: Teachers College Press, 1973), p. 8.

when under court orders to desegregate, the impression is conveyed that most of the more than nineteen million American school children bused are victims of schemes devised by social engineers. But the data show that in 1972 desegregation accounted for a mere 3 percent increase in busing.[13] What this means is that cries of massive busing are really aimed at integrated schools rather than at the issue of busing. As one angry mother from rural Alabama so aptly put it: "As long as we don't have niggers on there it's not busing. Busing is making white children get on with niggers."[14] There may be many valid arguments against school busing, but they are not the ones one usually hears. Furthermore, before the *Swann* decision one heard few complaints against busing. Prior to desegregation, busing was viewed as a means of improving the quality of education, especially in rural areas. It became necessary to transport students, often over long distances, to those consolidated schools where they could receive a better education. Furthermore, prior to *Brown v. Board of Education,* busing was commonplace among black students, who were often bused many miles (often as many as 100) because they were prohibited from attending school with white children. They frequently passed much better equipped white schools en route to the all-black school. And it was not at all uncommon to bus white children long distances and force black children to walk even longer distances, all in an effort to maintain segregated schools.

A longtime researcher of school integration, sociologist James Coleman maintains that what he calls forced busing is "a restriction of rights. We should be expanding people's rights, not restricting them."[15] The fallacious assumption in this argument is that in organized society individuals have unlimited rights. The very nature of social organization is such that some individuals will have their rights restricted for the good of the larger society. And certainly the inconvenience of a few who are bused for desegregation purposes can hardly compare with the larger societal good achieved by desegregation. The United States Commission on Civil Rights reports that "most school district officials feel that there has been an improvement in the quality of education for all school children" as a result of school desegregation. Furthermore, "In the past 10 years, desegregated schools have brought together more children of different races and ethnic groups than at any time in the history of the Nation."[16] Given the nature of American society it would be impossible to desegregate public schools without pupil transportation.

In addition to eliminating one-room schools through consolidation in rural areas, thereby permitting greater educational opportunities, busing has improved the quality of education in urban areas by relieving overcrowding and double sessions, and by the reduction of class sizes. In other words, cities and suburbs may now utilize school space and time more efficiently, thereby contributing to better education for all pupils. The myths surrounding what has become known as the school busing controversy are many. In an effort to dispel these myths, the NAACP Legal Defense and Educational Fund published, in 1972, an extensive study of busing entitled, *It's Not the Distance, It's the Niggers.*[17] Among its findings: Federal courts have not exceeded Supreme Court rulings and have not ordered "massive" or "reckless" busing in order to implement desegregation plans; increases in busing in some cities have occurred, but these are not always enormous and sometimes they are due to factors other than desegregation; busing is not harmful to children, and frequently serves to protect them; transportation for various school purposes is used to improve the educational program, not to undermine it; the cost of busing is minor and does not deplete resources of better schools.

OPEN ADMISSIONS

Whenever a program designed to make for greater democracy, and specifically to assist minorities, is introduced in any segment of American society there are likely to be strong objections, usually from those who have profited from the status quo. The introduction of open admissions in the City University of New York in 1970 caused a national uproar, with prophecies of the decline and ultimate death of the university. The reasons given for these forecasts were many, but the major one appeared to be that the influx of black and other minority students, all of whom were considered to be unqualified, would mean the destruction of academic standards, as was suggested by former vice-president Spiro Agnew.[18]

Other opponents of open admissions found additional reasons for their positions. For example, conservative Irving Kristol (himself a product of an open admissions system) has flatly declared that "open admissions will not work. Its promise is fraudulent. And both politicians and educators could pay

142

dearly for being implicated in this fraud."[19] He went on to predict that in a generation, "New York City's college system – traditionally one of the best in the nation – will have the educational status of an advanced high school." Here again the question of standards was raised. And sociologist Robert Nisbet bases his opposition, to a large extent, on remedial education as an integral component of open admissions. "I am convinced that high school level work can be taught successfully in the high school, not in the university under whatever name."[20]

In the spring of 1969 black and Puerto Rican students from City College waged a struggle to democratize the college and force it to reflect the changing character of New York City's population. A student strike resulted and the black and Puerto Rican students occupied South Campus and presented a list of five demands to the college.[21] These demands were that a separate school for black and Puerto Rican studies be established; that black and Puerto Rican freshmen be given a separate orientation program; that SEEK (Search for Education, Elevation, and Knowledge) students have a voice in setting guidelines, and in hiring and firing of all personnel; that the racial composition of all entering classes reflect the black and Puerto Rican population of New York City high schools; and that black and Puerto Rican history and the Spanish language be required of all education majors. In sum, black and Puerto Rican students were demanding that public higher education in New York City be democratized.

When public higher education in New York City was initiated in 1847 the chairman of the board of education made the following statement: "Open the doors to all. Let the children of the rich and the poor take their seats together and know of no distinction save that of industry, good conduct, and intellect."[22] The first institution to be established was the Free Academy, which became the College of the City of New York. All applicants were admitted, and tuition was free. Later several other colleges were added, and in 1961 they comprised what is now the City University of New York. Open admissions in New York City, then, is more than a century old. However, after World War I pressures became so intense that there were not enough classrooms to house all those who wanted to enter. Consequently, academic admissions standards were established in 1924. Admission to a unit in the system was contingent on an overall high school average of 72, and this was raised several times until it reached 85 in 1969.

But open admissions is not peculiar to New York; many state universities have always admitted all high school graduates in the state. In Ohio, for example, state law requires that all students who graduate from twelfth grade are entitled to admission to any college or university supported wholly or in part by the state.[23] The only limitation to admittance to public colleges or universities in Ohio is the ability to pay tuition.

In Nebraska, publicly supported colleges and universities admit all residents of the state graduating from accredited high schools.[24] These institutions admit students with deficiencies, which are to be corrected as soon as possible. Special efforts are made to attract low-income and minority students by recruiting them from high schools. It should also be noted that the attrition rate (which is quite high) is greatest among students who graduated in the bottom one-third of their high school classes, meaning, of course, minorities and the poor. And there is the question of financial assistance. Although the university has allocated funds to keep low-income and minority students in attendance, these funds are hardly adequate.

The state of California has long been considered to be a model for the nation in its open admissions policy at its various community colleges, senior colleges, and universities. Entrance is theoretically granted to all high school graduates through what is called "universal access." The state constitution expresses this sentiment by declaring that "a general diffusion of knowledge and intelligence [is] . . . necessary to the preservation of the rights and liberties of the people."[25] In an effort to provide "universal access," a three-tiered system of higher education has been provided, including the California community colleges, the California state universities and colleges, and the University of California.

The system operates in a stratified manner in which the nearly 100 community colleges are required by law to accept all California high school graduates and citizens over eighteen deemed "capable of profiting from the instruction offered." Within the system only community colleges are tuition free. The California state universities and colleges are obligated to admit the top third of all California high school graduating seniors. And the University of California must accept the top 12.5 percent of the state's high school graduates.

According to one source, the community colleges provide the only open access to postsecondary education.[26] For example, remedial courses are provided for all in need, and community leaders govern these schools. But these schools are largely middle class, as is the situation with the other units in the system. Low-income students tend to be channeled into vocational programs.

The community colleges of California come closer to providing "universal access" than do the state university system or the University of California system. For example, the University of California attracts students from relatively more well-to-do families, whereas the state university system and the community colleges provide for the middle class and the poor. In 1972, some 26.2 percent of the students in the University of California were from families with incomes in excess of $21,000. This figure compared with 13.2 percent in the state university, and 11.5 percent in the community colleges.[27] The ethnic breakdown is shown in Table 8.2.

It is clear that social class and ethnicity are correlated. This means that in California ethnic minorities and the poor do not

Table 8.2. *Ethnic representation in California's postsecondary educational system (in percentages)*

	Black	Chicano	Asian	Native American	White
Community colleges	8.4	7.9	3.4	1.2	77.9
State university	4.8	5.4	5.0	1.0	83.9
Univ. of California	3.6	3.2	7.3	0.6	85.2

Source: Seth Brunner, "Post Secondary Educational Opportunity in California," in David Rosen et al. (eds.), *Open Admissions: The Promise and the Lie of Open Access to American Higher Education* (Lincoln, Nebr.: Study Commission on Undergraduate Education and the Education of Teachers, 1973).

have equal access to postsecondary education as is the case for the middle and upper classes. It also means that middle- and upper-class students, having attended the most prestigious schools in the system, will be able to command the better-paying jobs, thereby perpetuating the system of inequality. One writer, familiar with the California system, concludes:

> Open access in California, long heralded as a reality, is an illusion. The system is rigidly stratified, with controls regulating who gets in. The potential of providing a diverse number of learning experiences in the various strata of the system has been squelched by the preservation of a status system. The "open door" in California leads to the basement, with the penthouse reserved for those who have always been privileged enough to accept."[28]

Many other states provide a variant of open admissions to students desiring postsecondary education, but as the California system demonstrates, the concept is often used to describe systems that are "democratic" in some respects but not in others. We now turn to an examination of the open admissions policy of the City University of New York. The experience of the City University with open admissions is in many ways unique, an attempt to establish a democratic system of education in which persons of all classes, races, religions, and nationalities would have the same opportunities for postsecondary education.

Open admissions had been part of the Master Plan of the City University for several years, but after the 1969 strike at City College it was decided that it should be put into effect in the fall of 1970. The university consists of nine senior colleges, eight community colleges, and a graduate center. These eighteen units accommodate some 170,000 students. In order to be admitted to a unit other than the Graduate Center, students must submit applications listing their first six choices. The students' transcripts are submitted to the University Application Processing Center, where the transcripts of all high school seniors are computerized.[29] Teams from the Office of Admissions Services visit each unit in the university system each March to determine the availability of spaces in each program of study (e.g., liberal arts, nursing). Programs that are in greatest demand are filled by students with the highest academic ranks. That is, any student with a high school grade point average of 80 or above or who ranks in the top one-half of his or her class is guaranteed a seat in a senior college. All others are likely to be admitted to one of the community colleges. This is hardly democratic, but all students applying are assured places in one of the university's units.

Financial assistance, based on family income, is provided students in the senior colleges by the SEEK program, and for students in the community colleges by the College Discovery program. Since the institution of tuition in 1975 other programs of loans and grants have been available, in keeping with the spirit of open admissions. In addition, each unit has testing facilities, a system of preregistration and registration advising, remedial courses (especially in English and mathematics), tutoring services, and academic advising.

A survey of students in attendance at both community and senior colleges in the university system was conducted for the 1975–76 academic year.[30] In the senior colleges, some 62.8 percent were white, 20.5 percent were black, and 11 percent were of Hispanic background. The community colleges enrolled 41.4 percent white students, 35.7 percent black students, and 18.2 percent Hispanic students. Therefore, it appears that black and Hispanic students are more likely than white students to be forced into the community colleges.

As is the case with open admissions in the California system of postsecondary education, the community colleges of the City University are more likely to enroll low-income students than the senior colleges. Some 17.8 percent of students in the community colleges were from families with annual incomes under $4,000, compared with 11.4 percent in the senior colleges. On the other extreme, 5.4 percent of all students in the community colleges were from families with incomes of $24,000 or over, compared with 11.6 percent of students in the senior colleges.

As is clear, open admissions programs, where practiced, vary widely. The City University has, in some ways, made the greatest strides but even there the system can only be considered undemocratic. However, as a key participant in the open admissions program at Hunter College described the process, "City University became a funnel into which people of all classes, races, religions, nationalities, and experiences were poured and out of which 'college students' emerged. This truly democratic attempt to equalize opportunity through education did not, in its planning stage, take into account the full extent of the task."[31]

A more critical point of view was expressed by one who has conducted research on the City University program. Open admissions, he writes,

> has not yet cracked the tracking system; it has not yet eliminated discrimination along racial and class lines; it has not yet cemented a respect for minority cultures and life experiences. And because institutions of higher education are part of a much more pervasive system, open admissions has not yet ended their complicity with that system's efforts to control and channel people in "proper" directions.[32]

Education, especially on the postsecondary level, is one of the areas in which black people have made greatest advances in the past two decades. But even here the progress is somewhat deceptive because although many more attend established senior colleges, they tend (some 46 percent) to be enrolled in community colleges. And in 1972 the majority of black students received associate degrees or others below the baccalaureate. There is some indication that community colleges are becoming institutions for the disadvantaged of the society. Furthermore, financial assistance is a serious problem for minority students. These students rely heavily on loans and scholarships, supplementing these by income from employment. With the fiscal policies of the Reagan administration, it is quite likely that large numbers of black students will be forced to terminate their schooling.

The transportation of pupils to achieve desegregation where white school officials have deliberately maintained dual school systems has become a major issue in public secondary education. The objections stem largely from white racist parents, whose arguments conceal their real motivation, namely, to keep the schools segregated. Many of the opponents of busing insist that all parents involved, black and

148

white, reject busing, but a recent (1981) Louis Harris poll found that a majority (54%) of all parents whose children are bused say the experience has been "very satisfactory." Of the national sample, 33 percent said busing has been partially satisfactory, and 11 percent felt it has not been satisfactory.[33] For black parents three-fourths (74 percent) felt that the experience had been very satisfactory. Busing must take its place as the biggest phony issue in decades, and the Reagan administration has predictably selected this as an alternative that must end.

Open admissions is an attempt to make postsecondary education more democratic. Few states have such programs in their senior colleges and universities, and where they exist they are not democratic. With the establishment of hundreds of community colleges to provide greater access for minorities and the poor, these colleges are often less well staffed and equipped than some of the better high schools. Community colleges have become places for minorities and the poor, and most of them do not live up to the promise of democratic education. Our educational institutions, it seems, are not living up to the professed American ideal of democracy.

BAKKE, WEBER, AND THE MYTH
OF REVERSE DISCRIMINATION

THE case of the *Regents of the University of California v. Allan Bakke* has been a critical one for minorities and women since 1973, when Bakke first applied for admission to the School of Medicine at the University of California at Davis. Bakke was rejected by the school in the spring of 1973 and again in the fall of 1974, as he had been at ten other medical schools to which he had applied.[1] After the second rejection, Bakke learned that the medical school maintained a special admissions policy setting aside 16 of the 100 first-year positions for members of economically and educationally disadvantaged minorities. At the urging of an administrator at the school he then retained a lawyer to file suit against the university, challenging the admissions policy on the grounds that it violated the equal protection clause of the Fourteenth Amendment. In other words, he charged the medical school with practicing "reverse discrimination," in that it gave preferential treatment to minorities.

The Yolo County (California) Superior Court ruled that the university's program was invalid in that it discriminated against Bakke because of his race. However, it did not order the medical school to admit him, and both the university and Bakke appealed. The California Supreme Court held, on September 16, 1976, that the university's affirmative action program was unconstitutional because it violated the equal protection rights of whites. The school was ordered to admit Bakke in the fall of 1977, but it was permitted to retain its admission policy until the United States Supreme Court could review the case. That review was granted in February 1977, and the decision was handed down June 28, 1978. By a five-to-four margin the Supreme Court ruled that the admissions program at the University of California at Davis was illegal because it was said to have violated Title VII of the Civil Rights Act of 1964. The minority declared that the admissions program, if administered properly, violated neither the Civil Rights Act of 1964 nor the equal protection clause of the Fourteenth Amendment.

THE DECISION

The *Bakke* case was of such significance that six separate opinions were written by the justices. Both Justices Thurgood Marshall and Harry Blackmun wrote dissenting opinions in strong language. For example, Justice Blackmun wrote:

> I suspect that it would be impossible to arrange an affirmative action program in a racially neutral way and have it be successful. To ask that this be so is to demand the impossible. In order to get beyond racism, we must first take account of race. There is no other way. And in order to treat some persons equally, we must treat them differently.[2]

Justice Marshall wrote:

> Today's judgment ignores the fact that for several hundred years Negroes have been discriminated against, not as individuals, but rather solely because of the color of their skins. It is unnecessary in 20th century America to have individual Negroes demonstrate that they have been victims of racial discrimination; the racism of our society has been so pervasive that none, regardless of wealth or position, has managed to escape its impact.
>
> I fear that we have come full circle. After the Civil War our government started several "affirmative action" programs. This Court in the *Civil Rights Cases* and *Plessey v. Ferguson* destroyed the movement toward equality. For almost a century no action was taken, and this nonaction was with the tacit approval of the courts. Then we had *Brown v. Board of Education* and the Civil Rights Acts of Congress, followed by numerous affirmative action programs of the type used by the University of California.[3]

But a majority of the justices concurred in the decision written by Justice Lewis F. Powell. In essence this decision invalidated the affirmative action program at the University of California at Davis, and ordered Bakke admitted. Justice Powell played a pivotal role in the decision, agreeing with four other justices that the race of an applicant may be taken into account as a factor in admissions to colleges and universities. He also agreed with a different four justices that the special admissions program at the university was invalid and that Bakke be admitted. Some excerpts from Justice Powell's opinion follow:

> In summary, it is evident that the Davis special admission program involves the use of explicit racial classification never before countenanced by this Court. It tells applicants who are not Negro, Asian, or "Chicano" that they are totally excluded from a percentage of the seats in an entering class. No matter how strong their qualifications, quantitative and extracurricular, including their own potential for contribution to educational diversity, they are never afforded the chance to compete with applicants from the preferred groups for the special admission seats.
>
> The fatal flaw in petitioner's preferential program is its disregard of individual rights as guaranteed by the Fourteenth Amendment.
>
> With respect to the respondent's entitlement to an injunction directing his admission to the Medical School, petitioner has conceded that it could not carry its burden of proving that, but for the existence of its unlawful admissions program, respondent still would not have been admitted. Hence, respondent is entitled to the injunction, and that portion of the judgement must be affirmed.[4]

The supporters of Bakke, by the positions they assumed, felt that the long history of racial oppression in the United States (as Justice Marshall pointed out in his dissent) was now behind us and that minorities had achieved parity with whites. Some even maintain that affirmative action and the gains of the 1960s have now tipped the scales in favor of minorities. It is therefore assumed that today everybody is equal under color-blind laws, and that everyone must compete equally on the basis of individual qualifications for every job and for every place in school.

SOME FACTS ABOUT *BAKKE* AND AFFIRMATIVE ACTION

Allan Bakke, a thirty-eight-year-old white engineer, applied for admission to the medical school at the University of California at Davis in 1973, along with 2,643 others, and in 1974, along with 3,737 others. He was rejected both times. The school accepts 100 students each year. Sixteen places are set aside for economically and educationally disadvantaged minority students. What the university never admitted is that each year the dean of the college sets aside several places for the sons and daughters of wealthy alumni. Yet the sixteen places set aside for minorities fall short of their 25 percent of the population of California.

The university never introduced evidence showing that thirty-six of eighty-four white students admitted in 1974 had lower test scores than did Bakke. Furthermore, the university did not admit that Bakke had been turned down by ten other medical schools, one of which had no minority admissions program, and three of which had fewer than 5 percent minority applicants.[5] And the university never admitted past discrimination, even though prior to its special admissions program, only three minorities had ever been admitted – one black and two Chicanos.

The increase in minority enrollment in professional schools peaked in 1973 and has stabilized in some fields and eroded in others. Of the forty medical schools with the most comprehensive affirmative action programs, twenty had ended their efforts while the Bakke case was in litigation. Lack of financial aid, tutoring, and support services is strangling those programs that still exist. Compared to the national average of one doctor for every 700 people, there is still only one black doctor for every 3,800 black people, a figure that has remained unchanged since 1930. There is only one Chicano doctor for every 30,000 Chicanos. Even with affirmative action, first-year minority enrollment in California medical schools in 1975–6 was only 15.8 percent, a low figure considering the 25 percent minority population in California.[6]

In a letter to the *New York Times*, deans and professors from medical schools around the country set forth reasons the Court should rule against Bakke.[7] Prior to 1968, first-year minority enrollments never exceeded 200, about 2 percent of the total first-year enrollment, and more than two-thirds of these places, were at Howard University and Meharry Medical School, both predominantly black. It was impossible for there to have been an increase in the acceptance of minority medical students until white medical schools began to open their doors to them, and this took place simultaneously with the 50 percent expansion in total first-year enrollments. Current first-year minority enrollment is about 8.2 percent, far below their 18 percent national representation, and has slipped in recent years.

The admissions policy of the medical school at the University of California at Davis has been attacked as representing "reverse discrimination" and has been accused of simply permitting unqualified students to enter the medical school. Rather than being an attempt to discriminate against Bakke and other nonminority students, the program was intended to include all groups. It is recognized that medical schools throughout the country have systematically discriminated against blacks, and the California program attempted to correct this pattern. It is because of such discrimination that President Johnson issued Executive Order 11246, setting forth affirmative action guidelines. Some critics maintain that the guidelines amounted to unwarranted federal intervention. If the federal government had not issued the guidelines, colleges and universities no doubt would have continued their policies of excluding, or accepting few, black students. Prior to the 1960s many major colleges and universities simply did not admit black students. It is the responsibility of the federal government to protect the rights of all citizens. Those who term affirmative action, as practiced at the University of California at Davis, reverse discrimination are perpetuating a cruel hoax because it was Afro-Americans who fought for and ultimately won a constitutional amendment prohibiting discrimination on the basis of race, and now that amendment has been used against them. Rather than discriminate against nonminorities the *Bakke* decision has served to strip minority people of the small gains they have achieved through long and difficult struggles.

With regard to the unqualified students charge, there is no evidence that those students admitted to the program at Davis were unqualified. Charges are leveled but no facts are presented. Although it is true that some of the minority students had lower grade point averages than those admitted through the regular procedure, each of the students was qualified to pursue a medical education. The university did not admit unqualified students. The second time Bakke was denied admission to the medical school more than 3,000 students applied. This certainly does not mean that the 2,900 rejected students were unqualified to become physicians.

If minority children were educated in a nonracist society, one that properly allocated educational resources at the primary and secondary levels, then the percentage of minorities in professional schools would naturally approximate the percentage of minorities in the society as a whole. Then special admissions programs would be unnecessary. But many factors enter into one's performance, especially on standardized tests. Take the Scholastic Aptitude Test, for example. Studies have shown, as Table 9.1 indicates, that SAT scores are correlated with students' family income.

Furthermore, several recent studies have demonstrated the absence of a correlation between test scores and the ability to function in graduate and professional schools or in one's profession. The Association of American Medical Colleges shows that blacks who had successfully completed their first two years of medical school had received lower scores on the entrance examination than whites who had flunked out of medical school.[8]

Those critics of affirmative action are shortsighted because government preference is not new to American life. There are special preferences for veterans, for the handicapped, and in the progressive income tax. To deny these preferences to the victims of centuries of oppression by the society can only be considered a gross act of cruelty.

In an editorial before the *Bakke* decision, the *New York Times* discussed "The Complaints of White Men." After admit-

Table 9.1. *SAT scores and family income*

SAT average score	Family's average income
750–800	22,425
700–749	21,099
650–699	19,961
600–649	18,906
550–599	17,937
500–549	16,990
450–499	16,139
400–449	15,240
350–399	14,068
300–349	10,352
250–299	9,865
200–249	7,759

Source: *The Bakke Case, Affirmative Action and Higher Education* (New York: Faculty Action, 1978), p. 20.

ting that its staff was largely white and male (a policy in the process of change), and enumerating the complaints of white men against affirmative action, the *Times* wrote: "We sensed the accumulating strength of the backlash while studying the *Bakke* case last summer. And if Mr. Bakke persuades the Supreme Court that race-conscious affirmative action at the Davis medical school of the University of California was illegal discrimination against him, then all forms of affirmative action would become instantly suspect and the subject of prolonged litigation. They would be abandoned in many places, quickly and tragically." The editorial continued: "Not only some abstract concept of justice but the well-being of the American community depends upon affirmative action that can help overcome the stigma and injury of the past." Finally: "To the complaint of white men that this [affirmative action] complicates their lives as a group, there is only one honest reply: Sure it does. But if they are being deprived to some extent, it is only in the sense that they are losing the opportunity which they would not have had without past discrimination."[9]

A word about affirmative action legislation. Such legislation was initiated in 1965 by executive order (11246), signed by President Lyndon Johnson, and another executive order (11375) was signed in 1967. Executive Order 11246 was amended to include the following:

> In signing a Government contract or subcontract in excess of $10,000 the contractor agrees that it "will not discriminate against any employee or applicant for employment because of race, color, religion, sex or national origin," and that it "will take affirmative action to ensure that applicants are employed and that employees are treated during employment" without regard to these factors. In the event of the contractor's noncompliance with the nondiscriminatory clauses of the contract, or with the rules and regulations of the Secretary of Labor, the contract may be cancelled, terminated or suspended in whole or in part and the contractor may be declared ineligible for further government contracts.[10]

Executive Order 11246 deals with two concepts: nondiscrimination and affirmative action. Nondiscrimination

> requires the elimination of all existing discriminatory conditions whether purposeful or inadvertent. A university contractor must carefully and systematically examine all of its employment policies to be sure that they do not, if implemented as stated, operate to the detriment of any persons on grounds of race, color, religion, sex or national origin. The contractor must also ensure that the practices of those responsible in matters of employment, including all supervisors, are nondiscriminatory.[11]

Affirmative action

> requires the contractor to do more than ensure employment neutrality with regard to race, color, religion, sex, and national origin. As the phrase implies, affirmative action often requires the employer to make additional efforts to recruit, employ and promote qualified members of groups formerly excluded, even if that exclusion cannot be traced to particular discriminatory actions on the part of the employer. The premise of the affirmative action concept of the Executive Order is that unless positive action is undertaken to overcome the effects of systemic

157

institutional forms of exclusion and discrimination, a benign neutrality in employment practices will tend to perpetuate the *status quo ante* indefinitely.[12]

The persons protected by the executive order include minorities (blacks, Spanish surnamed, Native Americans, Asians) and women. Affirmative action is a technique designed to promote equality and justice for women, especially in the work force of industries and in colleges and universities. Although some persons and groups viewed affirmative action as preferential treatment, in reality it is simply a tool to make employment practices fair ones. In the case of higher education, the attempt is to make certain that parity will exist between promotion of blacks in the general population and their employment at all levels of academia.[13]

Affirmative action programs are necessary because, given the nature of American society, without them rampant discrimination in employment and higher education would persist. Evidence to support this contention can be seen in the status of black people from Reconstruction to the present time. And even though the Fourteenth Amendment was meant to provide freedom for blacks, it was rarely used on their behalf until recent years. One might say then that the Fourteenth Amendment set the constitutional basis for affirmative action.

One writer has pointed out that since the Civil Rights Act of 1964, several court decisions have ordered employers and unions to engage in "ratio" hiring or "quota" relief to overcome the effects of past discrimination and to compel fairness in employment.[14] At the same time seniority systems that attempt to discriminate against minorities have been declared illegal. Although Title VII of the Civil Rights Act of 1964 was designed to eliminate discrimination in employment, in recent years the courts have gone beyond this and have ordered affirmative relief to ensure equality in employment. Thus, through the years the courts have upheld affirmative action as a legitimate means toward achieving racial equality.

AFTER THE *BAKKE* DECISION

The confusing decision of the Supreme Court in the *Bakke* case has had an unfortunate impact on affirmative action programs around the country. Indeed, even before the Court announced its decision, many organizations, fearful of what the decision would be, cut back on affirmative action programs. Others acted to curb affirmative action programs as soon as the decision was announced. Some examples:

Ohio construction contractors have obtained a preliminary injunction against some state projects set aside for minority contractors on the grounds that this is barred by *Bakke.*

Some white workers at one Aramco steel plant in Ashland, Kentucky, have brought suit to eliminate apprenticeship quotas set in the 1974 Consent Decree. The decree had been filed by the United Steelworkers Union, the government, and the steel companies, following pressure from activists. The agreement provided that 50 percent of new apprenticeship openings were to be filled by black, Hispanic, and women workers.

An antibusing organization in Los Angeles has taken the city to court on the grounds that "excessive busing" means a quota system, prohibited by *Bakke.*

In Richmond, Virginia, a redevelopment project utilizing one-fourth black workers is being reexamined in light of the *Bakke* decision.

In California, minority leaders view the decision as making it more difficult to keep minority workers from being fired en masse in the face of budget cuts mandated by Proposition 13.

The House of Representatives passed a bill to amend the Small Business Act that included the finding that blacks and Hispanics had been subjected to social and economic discrimination. The Senate blocked passage on the grounds of probable unconstitutionality.

Citing the *Bakke* case as precedent, a Los Angeles judge declared unconstitutional a recently passed federal law requiring that 10 percent of some government construction funds go to minority-owned companies. A similar ruling was rendered in Boston.

In New Jersey, ratio hiring to remedy police and fire department discrimination was ruled unconstitutional by the New Jersey Supreme Court.

A federal court declared that the use of quotas in the distribution of scholarship funds is impermissible.

In housing, the U.S. Supreme Court ruled that officials of a Chicago suburb (Arlington Heights) could refuse a building permit for a proposed apartment complex which would have had some black occupants. They argued that while this refusal was in fact discriminatory in its effect, it was necessary to show intent to discriminate.

THE *BAKKE* CASE, BLACKS, AND JEWS

The case of the *Regents of the University of California v. Allan Bakke* has been critical in black–Jewish relations since 1973, when Allan Bakke first applied for admission to the School of Medicine at the University of California at Davis. The *Bakke* case became one of the most controversial civil rights cases to come before the Supreme Court in many years, and more than sixty briefs, a record, were submitted for and against Bakke, with the vast majority (three-fourths) opposed. It is significant to note that not one Jewish organization filed a brief in support of the affirmative action program at the University of California at Davis, but many filed pro-Bakke briefs.[15] Those groups supporting the medical school's admission policy, that is, those filing friends of the court briefs, included the U.S. Department of Justice; civil liberties and civil rights groups; universities; black professional organizations; Asian-Americans, Hispanic, Native American, and other Third World organizations; Protestant religious groups; and several unions.

On the other hand, an astonishing combination of Jewish and right-wing organizations filed briefs in support of Bakke. Among the Jewish organizations opposed to the medical school's affirmative action program were the American Jewish Committee, the American Jewish Congress, the Anti-Defamation League of B'nai B'rith, the Jewish Labor Committee, and the National Jewish Commission on Law and Public Affairs. These organizations were joined in their support of Bakke by other white ethnic organizations, police and law and order groups, the Chamber of Commerce of the United States, and Young Americans for Freedom, among other organizations usually considered to be among the right wing.

Jewish organizations supported Bakke because of their opposition to "quotas" and their faith in "merit selection." For example, in its brief the Anti-Defamation League maintained that "the universities which for centuries set the style in excluding or restricting Jewish students and those of various other religions, racial and ethnic minorities, may again be able to do so, again in the name of enlightenment and diversity, if the decision [in favor of Bakke] is not affirmed."[16] And the American Jewish Committee declared that "the position of the University of California 'necessarily means that there is a proper proportion of each group in each profession or calling. Acceptance of this concept would profoundly damage the fabric of our society.'"[17]

Those opposing Bakke did so because of their convictions that the society has a special responsibility to those citizens who have been victims of racial oppression for centuries. For example, in its brief the American Civil Liberties Union held that "the A.C.L.U. believes that a nation which has engaged in centuries of subjugation, segregation and discrimination cannot afford to take seriously the exhortations of those who now insist that under no circumstances should we abide selection processes in which race counts in the calculus."[18] And the NAACP Legal Defense and Educational Fund maintained that "the critical fact about the special admissions policy is, we submit, that it neither had the intention nor effect of stigmatizing respondent as inferior or slurring him because of his race or color."[19]

The pro-Bakke coalition's position was perhaps best stated by the general counsel of the Anti-Defamation League: "We view the Court's decision as a significant victory in the effort to halt the use of quotas and their equivalent in admissions to colleges and graduate schools. In our view, however, it would, as a practical matter, seem difficult to allow race to be used as one factor in admissions without that factor eventually becoming the determining factor."[20] While maintaining that the organization supports affirmative action programs, the Anti-Defamation League apparently objects to race being a permissible consideration in such programs.

The position of those supporting the medical school's affirmative action program was perhaps best summed up in a statement issued by three black professional organizations, the National Medical Association, the National Dental Association, and the National Bar Association: "The fear of our associations is that the net effect of Bakke can be a negative one. The Bakke case dealt with medical schools, but dental and law schools with programs similar to the one at the University of California are in jeopardy if the case is improperly implemented."[21] The vast majority of minority organizations and leaders have condemned the decision as one opposed to the interests and aspirations of minority people.

The *Bakke* decision is likely to serve as a setback for minority people and the minuscule gains won in the last decade or so after long and protracted struggles. It calls for individualized treatment in admissions programs, thereby paving the way for massive subterfuge. Furthermore, it relies on the good-faith efforts of people and institutions long antagonistic to minority aspirations. When this is done, it is not difficult to envision the outcome: The decision is likely to be seen as a signal for other universities to cut back on affirmative action programs. And it opens the door for any disgruntled white applicant denied admission in future years to use it as a basis for legal action against a university.

As people of color know best, the *Bakke* decision is likely to have an adverse effect on minority aspirations. It allows for so many options that it will probably have the same effect as the massive resistance campaigns in the South after the *Brown* decision, forcing individual minority persons to file suit to attend desegregated schools. Because the *Brown* implementation decree called for desegregation to take place "with all deliberate speed," it placed the burden on the victims rather than those responsible for violating the law. That is how American society operates with regard to minority people.

Finally, it is cruel and ironic that Afro-Americans, who fought for and ultimately won the right to have a constitutional amendment prohibiting discrimination on the basis of race, should now have that amendment used against them. By supporting Bakke, several Jewish organizations elected to join the neoconservative movement geared toward stripping minority people of the minor gains achieved through struggle. One expects greater compassion from those who themselves have been victims of oppression.

AND THE CASE OF BRIAN WEBER

After the Supreme Court decision in the *Bakke* case it was assumed by many whites, especially conservatives, that the nation would return to business as usual on matters pertaining to race. In one case, that of the *United Steel Workers of America v. Weber*, a thirty-two-year-old white worker at Kaiser Aluminum's Gramercy, Louisiana, plant sued the company and the union, charging reverse discrimination. The plant and the union, in 1974, established an affirmative action program for minority and women employees. Since its opening in 1956 the company maintained that it never discriminated against blacks. But in the region in which the plant is located, the total work force is approximately 40 percent black. And for the first ten years of its existence, the work force at the plant was less than 10 percent black. Furthermore, for many years there were only about twenty blacks in a work force of 500.[22]

The United Steelworkers of America devised the affirmative action program in nationwide collective bargaining with Kaiser Aluminum and Chemical Corporation. This program called for an increase in black and female participation in higher-paying skilled jobs. Goals set to achieve this called for admitting blacks and women until they constituted 40 percent and 5 percent of the employees, respectively. These goals were to be accomplished by admitting workers to the training program on a fifty-fifty basis: one minority worker or woman to one white male.

Brian Weber applied for the special training program, but it was ruled that he had insufficient seniority to get one of the places reserved for whites.[23] However, two of the blacks admitted had less seniority than he did. Weber filed a grievance through the union, but that was denied. He then wrote the Equal Employment Opportunity Commission in New Orleans for a copy of the Civil Rights Act. After reading it he visited the commission's office and filed a formal complaint. The commission never got around to a hearing. In accordance with the law Weber was sent a letter six months later informing him that he had the right to sue, whereupon he filed a class action suit representing all the white workers at Kaiser. He brought a lawsuit in Federal District Court charging violation of Title VII of the Civil Rights Act. The district court held that the program was illegal because the black workers benefiting from the program had not themselves been the victims of discrimination.

The case was appealed and the United States Court of Appeals for the Fifth Circuit affirmed the lower court's ruling. It held that Title VII permitted affirmative action programs only to remedy discrimination against individual employees. The Supreme Court agreed in December 1978 to hear the case, and arguments were heard the following March. Weber's lawyer argued that Congress, in enacting the Civil Rights Act of 1964, made it unlawful for any employer to discriminate against any individual because of race. The lawyer for the union, on the other hand, maintained that the Congress "meant to outlaw not discrimination in its most literal meaning, but discrimination that is invidious in the context of racial bigotry."[24] He said that when Congress enacted Title VII it did not mean to prohibit voluntary affirmative action programs.

The Kaiser affirmative action program was supported not only by the company and the union, but by the federal government as well. In addition to dozens of labor unions, there were civil rights groups and womens' organizations. One group, the Affirmative Action Coordinating Center, submitted a brief opposing Weber signed by sixty-four different organizations. Weber, on the other hand, was supported by several right-wing organizations, the Anti-Defamation League of B'nai B'rith, and the Polish American Congress.

The *Weber* case, unlike that of *Bakke*, did not involve the equal protection clause of the Fourteenth Amendment to the Constitution. It did not involve the Constitution at all. The Supreme Court viewed the Kaiser plan as a voluntary agreement between private parties whose behavior is not regulated by the Constitution. Therefore, the justices limited themselves to the question of whether Congress meant to bar this kind of voluntary action when discrimination based on race was outlawed. Thus, it can be said that the two cases were qualitatively different.

The United States Supreme Court handed down its decision in the *Weber* case on June 27, 1979. Two of the justices did not participate, one because he had worked for Kaiser and the other because he had been ill at the time of oral arguments. In a decision of 5 to 2, the Court held that voluntary affirmative action plans, even those with numerical quotas, do not necessarily violate Title VII of the Civil Rights Act of 1964. Writing for the majority, Justice Brennan wrote, "It would be ironic indeed if a law triggered by a nation's concern over centuries of racial injustice and intended to improve the lot of those who had 'been excluded from the American dream for so long' constituted the first legislative prohibition of all voluntary, private, race-conscious efforts to abolish traditional patterns of racial segregation and hierarchy." He continued: "An interpretation that forbade all race-conscious affirmative action would bring about an end completely at variance with the purpose and must be rejected."[25]

Chief Justice Burger and Associate Justice Rehnquist issued dissenting opinions. The chief justice wrote that in enacting Title VII, "Congress expressly *prohibited* the discrimination against Brian Weber the Court approves now." He accused the majority of "totally rewriting a crucial part of Title VII to reach a desirable result."[26] Associate Justice William Rehnquist wrote that the majority opinion "introduces into Title VII a tolerance for the very evil that the law was enacted to eradicate, without offering even a clue as to what the limits of that tolerance may be." He concluded: "Quite simply, Kaiser's racially discriminatory admissions quota is flatly prohibited by the plain language of Title VII."

The *Weber* case was seen as a victory for minorities (especially blacks) and women, for if he had won the case in the Supreme Court it would have served to set back affirmative action programs for decades into the future. As it now stands it provides a vehicle for achieving economic justice for those who have suffered discrimination for centuries. Weber's charge that he had nothing to do with past discrimination against blacks, and consequently should not have been denied admission to the training program, was appropriately answered by an official of the Office of Federal Contract Compliance in the Department of Labor. He said: "The question is whether you give priority to a group that's been systematically deprived of opportunity while Brian Weber's parents and grandparents were not discriminated against. If someone has to bear the sins of the fathers, surely it must be their children."

The attempt of white people (federal officials, Supreme Court justices, employers, unions, and individuals) to turn back the clock to the days when black people in the United States were the open victims of discrimination in all social institutions, by eradicating affirmative action programs, is nothing more than the revival of the neoconservative movement sweeping the country (discussed in Chapter II). It is cruel to be so insensitive to a people who have suffered so long in the society and who have never received a just share of social rewards. And the notion of reverse discrimination is not a valid concept where affirmative action is concerned. It is a smoke screen thrown up by those who would perpetuate the subordinate position of blacks in the United States. Brian Weber maintains, "I don't like to see people get screwed. I've always had a feeling for people." If Weber is so concerned about justice for people one wonders why he did not act when black workers at Kaiser were relegated to the lowest positions in the plant. Having been there for a decade, he was aware that there were some 20 black employees out of a work force of 500. Weber was not so concerned about blacks being "screwed." And shortly after the establishment of the affirmative action program, he sued to have the program dissolved. It is difficult to have sympathy for Weber, for he is clearly concerned about himself and the 20 of his "buddies" he encouraged to join him in the lawsuit. Although he declares that he is not a racist, this is doubtful because, in his own words, he sees himself as the champion of his own rights and those of what he calls a silent majority: the *whites* who make up 81 percent of the local's 800 members. It should be added that although he is a union official, he does not represent the blacks at the plant.

The cry of "reverse discrimination" is, in some cases, an effort to distort the meaning of affirmative action, and its intent to provide equal employment opportunity. The critics of affirmative action programs insist that such programs violate the principle of meritocracy in favor of employing "unqualified blacks." As one writer analyzed the situation: "They equate 'reverse discrimination' against individual white males with the systematic discrimination against blacks." But white males are not being excluded from college admissions or from jobs in favor of blacks. One must conclude that allegations of reverse discrimination distort the practice of affirmative action and that most of these charges are based on racial bigotry.

X

BLACK EQUITY IN WHITE AMERICA

DURING the period of Reconstruction, following slavery, many promises were made to the newly freed slaves. These included commitments to racial equality and economic opportunity. But, within a short time these promises were either compromised, ignored, or abandoned. And in the years shortly following Reconstruction, black people were essentially returned to slavery in every respect but name. In a few years of Reconstruction in the South the former slaves made significant progress in education, politics, and economics, but in the short period of approximately one decade it was back to business as usual, meaning a return to hard-core white supremacy.[1]

There can be little doubt that in many ways the present period represents a second reconstruction for America's black population. Beginning with the Supreme Court decision in *Brown v. Board of Education* in 1954, some of the segregation and discrimination against blacks was relaxed for the first time in well over half a century. This was limited mainly to areas outside the South, and it was not until such legislation as the Civil Rights Act of 1964, the Voting Rights Act of 1965, and the Fair Housing Act of 1968 that substantial progress was made in eliminating segregation and discrimination. It should be noted here that this rather drastic change in race relations resulted from the protracted struggles of the black population. In addition to these legislative acts, the black population, especially the youths, demonstrated by means of rebellions in the Watts section of Los Angeles (1965), Newark and Detroit (1967), and throughout the country after the assassination of Martin Luther King (1968) that they were unwilling to continue to suffer the oppression that had been thrust upon them by racist white Americans. The federal legislation as well as the rebellions ultimately led to equality in principle for black Americans. In the years following these events significant progress was made in virtually all areas of American life.

After the assassination of John F. Kennedy in 1963, Lyndon B. Johnson, his successor, vowed to rid the society of its remaining practices of segregation and discrimination. But America's war of aggression in Vietnam meant that Johnson was required to devote more time and money to this misguided venture. Johnson was seen by black Americans as the second Abraham Lincoln, for he vigorously pursued a policy of equal rights for all. But many Americans and people the world over failed to understand the vigor with which the world's most industrialized nation prosecuted a war against a divided poor Third World country. Johnson was soon to learn that it is impossible to maintain a humane domestic policy while pursuing a war abroad. The wholesale disenchantment with Johnson because of the Vietnam War forced him to decline to seek reelection in 1968.

Johnson's presidency proved to enhance the civil rights of blacks. His successor, Richard Nixon, was not only unsympathetic to blacks, he was antagonistic. For example, one of his first acts as president was to attempt to slow the pace of school integration by announcing that his administration would rely less on fund cutoffs by the Department of Health, Education and Welfare to achieve integration in the schools, and more on the courts.[2] Such an approach would have made the courts rather than the Executive branch enforcers of the law. And, as was demonstrated in the early days after the *Brown* decision, it would have placed the burden of bringing lawsuits on the victims themselves. A Supreme Court ruling was required to inform Nixon that his plan was unacceptable. But this was only after his secretary of Health, Education and Welfare had intervened in the case of thirty-three Mississippi school districts that had developed desegregation plans acceptable to HEW.

In the meantime, Nixon had selected John Mitchell to be attorney general. Mitchell, who was to become a convicted felon, recommended that the Voting Rights Act of 1965 not be renewed. He proposed a substitute bill that would have sub-

168

stantially weakened the enforcement provisions. Mitchell's proposal passed the House of Representatives but failed in the Senate.[3]

Thus, the way was paved for a reversal of the trend toward equality for America's black population. The Watergate scandal, with all of the earmarks of fascism, brought the downfall of the Nixon administration. His vice-president, Spiro Agnew, an opponent of increased rights for blacks, had already been forced to resign after pleading *nolo contendere* to one count of income tax evasion in a case in which he was accused of accepting kickbacks from Baltimore contractors. In 1974 Nixon became the first American president to resign his office after the House Judiciary Committee voted to impeach him. He was replaced as president by Gerald Ford, a conservative but less vociferous than his predecessor.

Gerald Ford's tenure in office was a brief one, for he was to face the electorate in two years. He had retained most of the staff he inherited from Nixon, and although he did not have a record of active interest in civil rights, he did little to turn back the clock. But he also did little to enhance the rights of black people. In the election of 1976 he was opposed by a southerner, Jimmy Carter, who during the campaign had enlisted the support of most of the country's black leadership. Gerald Ford had angered the American voters when he abruptly pardoned Nixon for all crimes after having indicated that he would not. Ford lost the election to Carter.

The Carter administration, a moderate one, had promised to pursue the cause of civil rights for blacks. Black voters in a few key states strongly supported Carter, and with their assistance he became president. During his one term, the rights of black citizens became one of his major concerns, and from the beginning he appointed more blacks and other minorities to key positions than had any of his predecessors. Furthermore, through a variety of programs he attempted to reduce youth unemployment. But progress in civil rights was tempered with caution because the mood of the country was rapidly becoming more conservative. It is because of the resurgence of conservatism, and the perception of many voters that Carter was a liberal, that he lost the election of 1980 to Ronald Reagan, an old-line conservative. Indeed, a *New York*

Black equity in white America

Times/CBS national poll found that white people voted Republican because, among other reasons, they believed the Democratic party had been too concerned with blacks.[4]

Although it is perhaps too soon to evaluate his presidency, there can be no doubt about where Reagan stands on both domestic and foreign policy matters. Because the 1980 election also produced a Republican majority in the Senate, the ultraconservatives there have made it clear that on domestic matters (e.g., social welfare programs, busing, abortion, prayer in the schools, voting rights) they intend to return the country to what it was prior to the depression of the 1930s. And on foreign policy questions the administration assumed an extreme cold war posture immediately upon entering office. It is clear that, for black people, no civil rights legislation will be proposed, and attempts are being made to repeal much of the existing legislation.

For example, the police department of the city of Detroit instituted in 1974 a voluntary affirmative action plan to hire and promote equal numbers of blacks and whites. Detroit is a city of 1.2 million people, 63 percent of whom are black. In 1974 blacks accounted for only 18 percent of the police force. The plan was seen as a remedy for past discrimination. It requires that two lists be kept for promotion – one for blacks and one for whites. Promotions are made alternately from the two lists, so that blacks and whites are promoted in equal numbers until half of the police lieutenants are black. The plan was upheld by the United States District Court in Detroit and the Court of Appeals for the Sixth Circuit, but it was challenged by the Detroit Police Lieutenants and Sergeants Association. The case is now before the Supreme Court, and the Reagan administration, through the Justice Department, filed a brief on December 3, 1983, asserting that the plan was unconstitutional.[5] In so doing Reagan becomes the first of the last five presidents to fail to support affirmative action.

Having won a popular victory at the polls without black support, the president has proceeded to propose legislation opposing the rights of black people. In this endeavor he has the support of a few black conservatives such as Thomas Sowell, an economist at the Hoover Institution, and Walter Williams, also an economist, from Virginia Commonwealth

170

University. A token black person, Samuel Pierce, was appointed Secretary of Housing and Urban Development, one of the lesser posts in the cabinet.

Reagan has promised to "get government off the backs of people." By this he means that the federal government should play a minor role in the lives of citizens. What is considered by many white Americans to be too much government interference in their lives means the reverse for black people. It was the federal government that outlawed segregation and discrimination against blacks. Left to their own designs many states would no doubt have maintained their laws designed to oppress blacks and other minorities. White Americans might resent the role of the federal government in their lives, whereas black people, for the most part, welcome a strong role by the federal government. Furthermore, American blacks have long depended on the government for employment. By 1980 some 67 percent of all black professionals and managers, compared with 17 percent in the population as a whole, worked for the government. And among black administrators some 42 percent worked for the government.[6]

During the election campaign of 1980 and the first months of the Reagan administration racial violence flared around the nation. A few incidents. A former Nazi who was vehemently antiblack was arrested in October 1980 and linked to several murders of blacks, and in some cases, their white companions.[7] Joseph Paul Franklin was accused of the murder of two black men in Salt Lake City who were jogging with two white women. In Oklahoma City a black man and a white woman were murdered in the parking lot of a supermarket. Furthermore, Franklin was charged with the murders of two black men in Indianapolis and two black teenagers, killed as they walked along the railroad tracks in Cincinnati. Finally, he was charged with the murder of a black man and a white woman in Johnstown, Pennsylvania. So far he has been convicted of violating the civil rights of the two black men in Salt Lake City.

Joseph Christopher, a white soldier, was arrested at Fort Benning, Georgia, and charged with the murders of seven black men in Buffalo and four in New York City.[8] During a thirty-hour period in September 1980 four black males were gunned down in the Buffalo area. In October two black cab

171

drivers were found slain in the Buffalo area. Their hearts had been cut out after they died. And in December a black man was stabbed to death by a white man as he waited for a bus. Another black man was also stabbed, but survived the attack. Finally, in New York City four black men were stabbed to death by a white man, and two others were wounded, all in an eight-hour period. Joseph Christopher has been accused of all these incidents.

In March of 1981 three white men were arrested in Mobile, Alabama, for the murder of a nineteen-year-old black man. He disappeared on Friday night and his body was found Saturday morning hanging from a tree. This can only be called a lynching.

During the election campaign of 1980 and the first few months of the Reagan administration, the climate was such that it encouraged racial violence. Racist murderers apparently assumed that they were free to kill black people with impunity. At the same time military dictators in Latin America, long wary of the Carter human rights program, launched reigns of terror against the people. The president had let it be known that his human rights campaign would be confined to socialist countries.

Inasmuch as the Republicans won a majority of seats in the Senate in the 1980 election, several right-wing senators became chairmen of important committees. Reagan had announced that his administration would fundamentally alter American society. These right-wingers were eager to assist in the task, especially where programs affected the lives of blacks and the poor. One such person is Strom Thurmond, the chairman of the important Senate Judiciary Committee and a presidential candidate on the segregationist States' Rights (Dixiecrat) party ticket in 1948. Thurmond has announced that he is planning major legal and constitutional changes for the country. He illustrated his intent by establishing a Security and Terrorism Subcommittee, whose function is the same as former witch-hunting committees concerned with the investigation of so-called subversives.

Thurmond's plan for America includes many changes affecting blacks.[9] He is seeking either legislation or a constitutional amendment to ban school busing. He favors repeal of the Voting Rights Act of 1965, which many consider the most successful civil rights legislation in the nation's history. In addition, Thurmond advocates the reestablishment of the death penalty; a constitutional amendment to permit prayers in public schools; a constitutional amendment to ban abortions; and the virtual abolition of the Freedom of Information Law.

Strom Thurmond is but one of many right-wing conservatives in high positions in government. Acting alone he could do little, but there are many like him in both the House of Representatives and the Senate. American voters, in their enthusiasm for Ronald Reagan, rejected several liberal members of Congress and replaced them with conservatives. And from all indications the vast majority of white Americans approve of Reagan and his fellow conservatives.

In its zeal to turn back the clock on social service programs, the Reagan administration is making life difficult for the poor, and blacks are disproportionately poor. All agencies in the federal government, except the Defense Department, will suffer from cutbacks, but those social programs affecting black people will be hardest hit. The Reagan cutbacks include $1.5 billion from the school lunch program, which was designed to provide nutritious lunches for children whose parents could not provide them. The food stamps program is projected to lose $1.6 billion (24.3 percent) under the Reagan administration. Designed to supplement the food purchasing power of the poor, this program has enabled many poor people to provide more nutritious meals for their families. In each of these cases black people, as a group, will suffer more than whites.

As if to demonstrate its contempt for blacks and other poor people, the Reagan administration plans to cut $1.1 billion from the Medicaid budget. This means that the inadequate health care services for the poor will either be curtailed or eliminated. Poor people living in areas without municipal health care services will simply not be able to afford medical care. And it is lamentable that in a society in which corruption and greed are rampant, all funds for legal services for the poor will be terminated. The Legal Services Corporation will be abolished on the assumption that poor citizens have no right to government-provided legal services. The elimination of the Legal Services Corporation is a serious one because in complicated situations most poor people simply do not know their legal rights. The corporation is one of the most successful programs, and this, in part, is the reason for its elimination.

Reagan would reduce funds by 25 percent for all elementary and secondary education programs. This comes at a time when a significant proportion of high school graduates leave school functionally illiterate. Schools in central cities, attended largely by blacks and other minorities, will be hardest hit. And this comes at a time when the quality of education is already declining. A program that especially affects black teenagers and young adults, and one that has had a measure of success, is that provided by the Comprehensive Employment and Training Act. It provides both employment and job training for the hard-core unemployed, and black youth are three times as likely to be unemployed as whites. This means that hundreds of thousands of young black people will spend their lives without work, subsisting by whatever means they can devise.

Altogether budget cuts for social service programs amount to some $48.6 billion. These cuts mainly affect the poor, the elderly, the unemployed, and the handicapped. Funds cut from these programs will be transferred to the Defense Department, the one department in the federal government that will have its appropriations increased. As of 1981 the military budget was approximately $173 billion, but the administration proposed to increase the appropriation to $226.3 billion, an increase of more than $53 billion in one year.[10] Furthermore, the military budget will be increased to $367.5 billion by 1986. In all, the administration proposes to spend $1.3 trillion on the Defense Department in the next five years.

Through its budget proposals the Reagan administration has clearly indicated where its priorities lie: making weapons of war instead of assisting those citizens who cannot help themselves. Given the nature of American society, it is clear that the primary victims of this punitiveness will be blacks, the poor, and other minorities.

The Reagan administration maintains that it is not anti-black, and Vice-President George Bush told members of the

May 1981 graduating class from Howard University that the administration has their best interests at heart. However, the reality appears to be that in many cases race is a major consideration. For example, the preceding administration had signed a contract for $99,000 with Delta Sigma Theta sorority, a black women's public service organization. The contract was to help train junior high school age pregnant teenagers and get them back in school. This contract is not being honored by the Reagan administration.[11] The administration also cut off funds for the A. Philip Randolph Educational Fund, a project that had placed some 2,500 young blacks in private-sector jobs in two years.

The same fate awaited Operation PUSH (People United to Serve Humanity): Its $2 million grant from the Department of Labor was cancelled. Each of these programs operated almost exclusively for the benefit of black Americans, and the effect of these cuts intensifies racial tensions, and undermines black community leadership.

While members of the administration claim that they are not antiblack, one would have to conclude otherwise if one compares actions with pronouncements. As a group black people are among the most needy in the society, and when budget cuts fall most heavily on social service programs blacks will suffer in disproportionate numbers. What the administration fails to understand is that if black people are treated as second-class citizens they have the numbers to make the society a difficult place in which to live. If Reagan thinks that the transition from a society in which efforts were being made to ameliorate racist practices to one in which racism is fashionable will not be met by resistance, he is likely to be in for a rude awakening. There is no possibility that blacks will suffer the fate today that they were forced to do during Reconstruction. If the government itself oppresses its citizens, then it can expect them to respond with all the resources at their command. The 1980s are radically different from the 1880s.

Although the 26.4 million blacks are less than 12 percent of the total population, they make up one-third of those who receive food stamps, Medicaid, and live in public housing. Furthermore, they make up about one-half of those who receive Aid to Families with Dependent Children. At the same time, only about 8 percent of those receiving Social Security retirement benefits are black, as are 9 percent of those receiving Medicare, and 10 percent of those receiving veterans' compensation and pensions. Those programs in which blacks are underrepresented will be retained with no cuts or only minor ones through what Reagan calls the "safety net."[12] Although he maintains that racism is not involved in the budget cuts, one can only wonder, for as Table 10.1 illustrates, the programs that have been of greatest assistance to blacks are those most seriously affected by the budget cuts.

It is understandably difficult for blacks not to see these proposed cuts as racist in nature. The President has said that in five or six years the free enterprise economy will provide meaningful employment for all Americans. In the interim what are the poor expected to do?

Table 10.1. *Blacks' share of public assistance and proposed budget cuts*

	Black share (%)	Proposed cut (%)
Social Security retirement and survivors' insurance	8.1	6.0
Medicare	9.3	2.0
Veterans' compensation and pensions	10.0	0
Supplemental Security Income	27.4	0
Aid to Families with Dependent Children	44.4	11.0
Food stamps	34.2	24.3
CETA public service jobs	33.0	90.8
Medicaid	34.9	5.0
Public housing	36.0	34.8
Social Security disability	14.9	7.2
Education for the disadvantaged	34.5	—
Extended unemployment insurance	15.0	15.4

Source: David Rosenbaum, "Blacks Would Feel Extra Impact from Cuts Proposed by President," *New York Times*, June 2, 1981, p. B11.

Black equity in white America

The notion that blacks have been advancing too rapidly is fueled by those social scientists (black and white) who, in their shortsightedness, declared in the 1970s that race was no longer a crucial variable in American life. They could not foresee the tide of conservatism that would sweep Ronald Reagan into office in 1980. Rather, they operated on the faulty notion of the meaning of race in American society. Change in this area comes about slowly, for antiblack prejudice is deeply rooted in the society. And to focus on isolated instances of black progress, ignoring the plight of most black citizens, is naive. In order to gauge black progress it is necessary to evaluate each institution in the society in relationship to others, for they are interrelated.

For example, the percentage of black students enrolled in institutions of higher education has more than doubled in the last decade. But these students tend to be clustered in community colleges, where the education they receive is frequently equivalent to that of some high schools. Furthermore, the surge in college enrollment has had little, if any, effect on overall black unemployment, which has averaged at least twice the rate of white unemployment for several decades. Because they generally hold low-status occupations, their earnings lag far behind those of white workers. Black median family income is approximately three-fifths that of white families. These data hardly support the exaggerated claims of black progress, and they illustrate the fallacy of a single indicator of change in the realm of race relations.

It must be admitted that black people made significant strides during the civil rights movement of the 1960s, but these gains only marginally affected the daily lives of most black families. Most of these families exert an exceptional amount of time and energy attempting to earn a living in an era of high inflation and high unemployment. These are working-class families whose lives were hardly touched by the civil rights movement. The small black middle class did expand during this period, but hardly to the extent reported in some of the recent literature on the subject. Furthermore, these reports do not take into account the expanding economic gap between blacks and whites.

The Reagan administration has given increased impetus to

177

the conservative movement in the United States, ranging from such neofascist groups as the Ku Klux Klan to the Moral Majority. Other groups include the American Conservative Union, the Conservative Caucus, Young Americans for Freedom, and the Christian Voice. These groups thrive on discontent, insecurity, and resentment. Their major interest in black people appears to be in maintaining the status quo. A conservative author writes: "While it would be inaccurate to attribute overt racism to much of the New Right, the appeal to fears about busing and quotas and welfare can play on racial anxieties."[13]

Given the present state of the decline in race relations in the United States, what can one say about the future? Above all, the prospects for black equity in the near future are not good. The opponents of greater civil rights for blacks appear to be well entrenched in policy-making positions. They seem to be determined to return to an era when improved civil rights for blacks was not an issue for discussion, to say nothing of action. The civil rights movement of the 1960s awakened America's black population to the need for struggle on all fronts, utilizing a variety of techniques. There is little likelihood that they will permit a reversal of the gains that have been made. Nevertheless, black people in the United States face a bleak future, for as a powerless minority they have few resources.

Perhaps the most serious problem facing black Americans is in the realm of economics. The civil rights movement was effective in achieving widespread school desegregation, voting rights, and desegregation in places of public accommodation. And although affirmative action improved job opportunities, especially for the middle class, the civil rights movement never really addressed itself to basic economic issues. If progress is to be made in the general status of blacks, economic advancement is crucial. Hundreds of thousands of black families are forced to live at or below the poverty level, and additional hundreds of thousands of black youths face the prospect of living their lives without ever entering the labor force. These are the types of black youths responsible for the rebellions in 1965, 1967, and 1968. If conditions for them do not improve, it is possible that they will make life in urban America difficult, to put it mildly.

Black equity in white America

The Reagan administration, with its emphasis on spending hundreds of billions of dollars for warfare in an effort to "contain communism" at the expense of domestic social programs, is threatening the domestic tranquillity of the country. The current administration like most of the rich it represents and serves, fails to understand the poor and is apparently unsympathetic to their plight. As long as conservatism dominates the country, there can be no progress in the area of race relations.

NOTES

CHAPTER I

1 U.S. Commission on Civil Rights, *Twenty Years After Brown: Equality of Educational Opportunity* (Washington, D.C.: Government Printing Office, 1974), p. 89.
2 Department of Labor, *The Negro Family: The Case for National Action* (Washington, D.C.: Government Printing Office, 1965).
3 Ibid., p. 5.
4 Lee Rainwater and William Yancey (eds.), *The Moynihan Report and the Politics of Controversy* (Cambridge, Mass.: MIT Press, 1967), p. 130.
5 Ibid.
6 Daniel P. Moynihan, "Memorandum for the President," *New York Times*, March 1, 1970, p. 69.
7 Nathan Glazer and Daniel Moynihan, *Beyond the Melting Pot* (Cambridge, Mass.: MIT Press, 1963), p. 53.
8 Nathan Glazer, *Affirmative Discrimination: Ethnic Inequality and Public Policy* (New York: Basic Books, 1975), pp. 67, 72.
9 Ben J. Wattenberg and Richard Scammon, "Black Progress and Liberal Rhetoric," *Commentary*, April 1973, p. 35.
10 Robert B. Hill, *The Illusion of Black Progress* (Washington, D.C.: National Urban League Research Department, 1978), pp. 19–24.
11 Ibid., p. 22.
12 Robert W. Fogel and Stanley L. Engerman, *Time on the Cross: The Economics of American Negro Slavery*. 2 vols. (Boston: Little, Brown, 1974).
13 The comments that follow draw heavily on Pinkney's review of this work, which appeared in *The Urban League Review*, vol. 1 (spring 1975), pp. 50–3.
14 Thomas Sowell, "Are Quotas Good for Blacks?" *Commentary*, June 1978, pp. 39–43. See also Sowell's *Affirmative Action Reconsidered: Was it Necessary in Academia?* (Washington, D.C.: American Enterprise Institute for Public Policy Research, 1975).

Notes

15 Sowell, "Are Quotas Good for Blacks?" p. 42.
16 Ibid., p. 43.
17 Richard B. Freeman, *Black Elite: The New Mar Educated Black Americans* (New York: McGraw-H
18 Chicago: University of Chicago Press, 1978.
19 Ibid., p. 1.
20 Ibid., p. 120.
21 Ibid.
22 Ibid., p. 151. Emphasis added.
23 Ibid., p. 152.
24 Ibid., p. 153.
25 Arthur Jensen, "How Much Can We Boost IQ and Scholastic Achievement?" *Harvard Educational Review*, winter 1969, pp. 1–123.
26 Richard Herrnstein, *IQ in the Meritocracy* (Boston: Little, Brown, 1973).
27 See, for example, Robert P. Althauser and Sidney S. Spivack, *The Unequal Elites* (New York: Wiley, 1975); Faustine Childress Jones, *The Changing Mood in America: Eroding Commitment?* (Washington, D.C.: Howard University Press, 1977); National Urban League, *The State of Black America 1979* (New York: National Urban League, 1979); Dorothy Newman, Nancy Amidei, Barbara Carter, Dawn Day, William Kruvant, and Jack Russell, *Protest, Politics, and Prosperity: Black Americans and White Institutions, 1940–1975* (New York: Pantheon Books, 1978).

CHAPTER II

1 In conservative thinking, the need for acceptance of the authority of institutions is foremost. Change, especially rapid change, is often viewed as dangerous and is appropriate in the conservative's view only when it fits established traditions. Conservatism places society first, as having an independent existence from the individuals who are a part of it. Society and its institutions progress through time and individuals have no prior claims and no rights except those society gives them in furtherance of their needs. Human beings are seen as unequal and needing a structured pattern of order.
2 *Gallup Opinion Index* (Princeton, N.J.: Gallup Poll, 1981), p. 178.
3 John Case, *Understanding Inflation* (New York: Penguin Books, 1982), p. 16.
4 *Gallup Opinion Index* (Princeton, N.J.: Gallup Poll, October 11–14, 1974), p. 31; (October 15–18, 1982), p. 22.

Notes

Susan Coughlin, *The Politics of Energy* (Washington, D.C.: Department of Energy, 1977).

6 Daniel Yankelovich, *New Rules: Searching for Self-fulfillment in a World Turned Upside Down* (New York: Random House, 1981), and Christopher Lasch, *The Culture of Narcissism* (New York: Norton, 1978).

7 Theodore White, "Summing Up," *New York Times Magazine,* April 25, 1982, pp. 74, 76, 78.

8 Michael Crozier, Samuel P. Huntington, and Jaji Watanuki, *The Crisis of Democracy* (New York: New York University Press, 1975).

9 Ibid., p. 7.

10 Ibid.

11 *Public Papers of the President of the United States,* Book 1–January 20–June 24, 1977 (Washington, D.C.: General Services Administration, 1977) pp. 1–4.

12 *Washington Post,* January 5, 1979, p. A2.

13 *New York Times,* May 21, 1979, p. 1.

14 *Gallup Opinion Index* (Princeton, N.J.: Gallup Poll, February 2–5, 1979), p. 23.

15 Laurence H. Shoup, *The Carter Presidency and Beyond* (Palo Alto, Calif., 1980), p. 185.

16 *Gallup Opinion Index,* 1979, p. 21.

17 Lester C. Thurow, *The Zero-Sum Society* (New York: Basic Books, 1980), p. 12.

18 An example of this was the 1975 fiscal crisis in New York City where in a "liberal" city, black males, who were 11 percent of the work force, accounted for 13 percent of the decline. Unpublished Data: Department of Personnel, New York City, 1982.

19 Kenneth M. Dolleare, *Directions in American Political Thought* (New York: Wiley, 1969).

20 Fred Hirsch, *Social Limits to Growth* (Cambridge, Mass.: Harvard University Press, 1976).

21 *The Washington Post,* April 28, 1983. Emphasis added.

22 The argument was not new. Nathan Glazer, one of the neoconservatives discussed later, presented essentially the same argument with similar wording in 1975. A similar argument can also be found in George Gilder's *Wealth and Poverty,* a favorite book of many Reagan administrators. (New York: Basic Books, 1981).

23 Belle Hooks, *Ain't I A Woman: Black Women and Feminism* (Boston: South End Press, 1981).

24 American Telephone & Telegraph Company, U.S. Court of Appeals, Third Circuit 1977, 566 F.2nd 167, 14 FEP.

25 There are conflicting views in social science research about affirmative action programs and black gains. However, there is general agreement that, to a limited degree, they assisted younger, well-educated blacks.

26 Christopher Lasch, *The Culture of Narcissism;* Robert LeKachman, "Between Apostles and Technicians," in Irving Howe and Michael Harrington (eds.), *The Seventies: Problems and Proposals* (New York: Harper & Row, 1971), pp. 74–9; Daniel Yankelovich, *New Rules.*

27 Alan Crawford, *Thunder on the Right: The "New Right" and the Politics of Resentment* (New York: Pantheon Books, 1980), p. 44.

28 *Record* (Washington: Federal Election Committee Nov. 1982), vol. VIII, no. 2, p. 5.

29 Crawford, *Thunder on the Right,* pp. 44–5.

30 *U.S. News and World Report,* April 4, 1983, p. 36.

31 *Gallup Opinion Index,* January 30–February 21, 1981, p. 61.

32 *U.S. News and World Report,* September 15, 1980, p. 24.

33 Frances Fitzgerald, "The Triumphs of the New Right," *New York Review of Books,* November 19, 1981, vol. XXVIII, no. 18, p. 20.

34 Ibid.

35 *The New York Times,* "Small Gifts to Allow G.O.P. to Outspend Foes in Fall," July 20, 1980.

36 Ibid.

37 Crawford, *Thunder on the Right,* p. 45.

38 *New York Times,* June 2, 1980, p. B11.

39 *Washington Post,* January 17, 1982, p. A2.

40 *Time,* September 14, 1981, p. 36.

41 Crawford, *Thunder on the Right,* p. 4.

42 Crawford, *Thunder on the Right,* p. 5.

43 Ibid., p. 245.

44 *New York Times,* February 10, 1980, p. E10.

45 *New York Times,* October 15, 1980, p. A18.

46 *Time,* September 28, 1981, p. 27.

47 *New York Times,* September 2, 1981, p. A16.

48 Thomas Ferguson and Joel Rogers, *The Hidden Election: Politics and Economics in the 1980 Presidential Campaign* (New York: Pantheon Books, 1982), p. 5.

49 Ibid., p. 3.

50 *New York Times,* March 9, 1983, p. A18.

51 Peter Steinfels, *The Neo Conservatives* (New York: Simon & Schuster, 1979), p. 7.

52 Daniel Moynihan, *Maximum Feasible Misunderstanding* (New York: Free Press, 1969), p. 170.

Notes

53 Ibid., p. 136.

54 Irving Howe, "The Decade that Failed," *New York Times Magazine*, September 19, 1982, p. 43.

55 Irving Kristol, "On Corporate Capitalism in America," in Nathan Glazer and Irving Kristol (eds.), *The American Commonwealth–1976* (New York: Basic Books, 1976), p. 134.

56 Irving Kristol, *Two Cheers for Capitalism* (New York: Basic Books, 1978), p. 145.

57 Kristol, *Two Cheers for Capitalism*, p. 183. Emphasis added.

58 *New York Times*, December 28, 1980, p. E5.

59 Nathan Glazer, *Affirmative Discrimination: Ethnic Inequality and Public Policy* (New York: Basic Books, 1975).

60 Ibid., p. 201.

61 Peter Steinfels, *The Neo Conservatives*, p. 1.

62 *The Gallup Index*, 1981, p. 184.

CHAPTER III

1 Karl Marx and Friedrich Engels, *The Communist Manifesto* (New York: Monthly Review Press, 1964), pp. 2–3.

2 Mao Tse-tung, *Quotations from Chairman Mao Tse-tung* (Peking: Foreign Languages Press, 1966), p. 10.

3 Theodore Draper, *The Rediscovery of Black Nationalism* (New York: Viking Press, 1970), pp. 63–4.

4 See Alphonso Pinkney, *Red, Black, and Green: Black Nationalism in the United States* (Cambridge: Cambridge University Press, 1976), chap. 6.

5 Judith Stein, "'Of Mr. Booker T. Washington and Others': The Political Economy of Racism in the United States," *Science and Society*, winter 1974–75, p. 463.

6 *Chicago Tribune*, November 11, 1967.

7 M. F. Ashley Montagu, *Man's Most Dangerous Myth: The Fallacy of Race* (New York: Harper and Brothers, 1952), p. 85.

8 John W. Cell, *The Highest Stage of White Supremacy: The Origins of Segregation in South Africa and the American South* (Cambridge: Cambridge University Press, 1982).

9 Harold M. Baron, "The Web of Urban Racism," in Louis Knowles and Kenneth Pruitt (eds.), *Institutional Racism in America* (Englewood Cliffs, N.J.: Prentice-Hall, 1969), pp. 134–76.

10 Robert Blauner, *Racial Oppression in America* (New York: Harper & Row, 1972), p. 146.

11 Donald L. Noel (ed.), *The Origins of American Slavery and Racism* (Columbus, Ohio: Charles E. Merrill, 1972).

Notes

12 Robert Staples, *Introduction to Black Sociology* (New York: McGraw-Hill, 1976), pp. 15–16.

13 Gunnar Myrdal, *An American Dilemma* (New York: Harper and Brothers, 1944), pp. 69–70.

14 Joseph W. Scott, *The Black Revolts: Racial Stratification in the U.S.A.* (Cambridge, Mass.: Schenkman, 1976), p. 59.

15 Earl Ofari, "Marxism, Nationalism, and Black Liberation," *Monthly Review*, March 1971, pp. 25, 29–30.

16 Joel Kovel, *White Racism: A Psychohistory* (New York: Random House [Vintage Books], 1971), p. 31.

17 George Fredrickson, *White Supremacy* (New York: Oxford University Press, 1981), p. 226.

18 E. Franklin Frazier, *Race and Culture Contacts in the Modern World* (Boston: Beacon Press, 1957), p. 210.

19 Stephen Steinberg, *The Ethnic Myth* (Boston: Beacon Press, 1981).

20 Robert Staples, "Tom Bradley's Defeat: The Impact of Racial Symbols on Political Campaigns," *The Black Scholar*, fall 1982, pp. 37–45; Tom Wicker, "Dissecting an Election," *New York Times*, February 18, 1983, p. A31.

21 W. E. B. Du Bois, *The Souls of Black Folk* (Chicago: McClurg, 1904), p. 13.

CHAPTER IV

1 Robert Blauner, *Racial Oppression in America* (New York: Harper and Row, 1972), p. 11.

2 *Atlanta Constitution*, June 29, 1979.

3 William Graham Sumner, *Folkways* (Boston: Ginn, 1906), p. 77.

4 Lee A. Daniels, "In Defense of Busing," *New York Times Magazine*, April 17, 1983, pp. 34ff. See also Jack Greenberg, *Race Relations and American Law* (New York: Columbia University Press, 1959).

5 Angus Campbell, *White Attitudes Toward Black People* (Ann Arbor, Mich.: Institute for Social Research, 1971).

6 "A Study of Attitudes Toward Racial and Religious Minorities and Toward Women" (New York: Louis Harris and Associates, 1978).

7 Ibid., p. 27.

8 Ibid., pp. 9–10.

9 Campbell, *White Attitudes*, p. 8.

10 *A Study of Attitudes*, p. 15.

11 Ibid., p. 16.

12 Ibid., p. 34.

13 Campbell, *White Attitudes,* p. 133.
14 *A Study of Attitudes,* p. 57.
15 Campbell, *White Attitudes,* p. 137.
16 Ibid., p. 136.
17 Joe R. Feagin and Clairece Feagin, *Discrimination American Style: Institutional Racism and Sexism* (Englewood Cliffs, N.J.: Prentice-Hall, 1978), pp. 20–1.
18 William Harris and Judith Levy, *The New Columbia Encyclopedia* (New York: Columbia University Press, 1975), p. 1,505.
19 *New York Times,* May 27, 1979, p. 26.
20 *New York Times,* May 28, 1979, p. A8.
21 Tom Wicker, "New Life for the Klan," *New York Times,* March 18, 1979, sec. 4, p. E21.
22 *New York Times,* July 7, 1979, p. 6.
23 *New York Times,* July 9, 1978, p. 26.
24 A. Pinkney, *Red, Black, and Green: Black Nationalism in the United States* (Cambridge: Cambridge University Press, 1976), p. 86.
25 *New York Times,* July 24, 1979, p. A10.
26 Alan Paton, "The Negro in America Today," *Colliers,* October 29, 1954, p. 70.
27 Department of Housing and Urban Development, *How Well Are We Housed: Blacks* (Washington, D.C.: Office of Policy Development and Research, 1976).
28 *New York Times,* April 17, 1978, p. A6.
29 *New York Times,* June 9, 1979, p. A12.
30 Ibid.
31 Ianthe Thomas, "Old Justice in the New South," *Village Voice,* April 24, 1978, pp. 13–14.
32 Bureau of the Census, *The Social and Economic Status of the Black Population in the United States: An Historical View, 1790–1978* (Washington, D.C.: Government Printing Office, 1979).
33 Ibid., p. 122.
34 Ibid., pp. 124–5.
35 *New York Times,* April 10, 1978, p. 1.
36 Ibid., p. D8.
37 *The State of Black America 1979* (New York: National Urban League, 1979), p. 26.
38 Ibid., p. 27.
39 Ibid., pp. 28–9.
40 *New York Times,* April 13, 1978.
41 *New York Times,* May 25, 1978, p. A20.
42 *New York Times,* June 11, 1979, p. B5.

Notes

43 *The Police and Their Use of Fatal Force in Chicago* (Chicago: Law Enforcement Study Group, 1972).

44 *New York Times,* December 22, 1978, p. A23.

45 *New York Times,* March 5, 1977.

46 *New York Times,* June 2, 1979, p. 6.

47 *Report of the National Advisory Commission on Civil Disorders* (New York: Bantam Books, 1968), p. 2.

48 Stokely Carmichael and Charles Hamilton, *Black Power: The Politics of Liberation in America* (New York: Random House [Vintage Books], 1967), p. 4.

CHAPTER V

1 Richard B. Freeman, *Black Elite: The New Market for Highly Educated Black Americans* (New York: McGraw-Hill, 1976), p. xx.

2 Ibid., p. 1.

3 William J. Wilson, *The Declining Significance of Race: Blacks and Changing American Institutions* (Chicago: University of Chicago Press, 1978), p. 1.

4 Ibid., p. 23.

5 Ibid., p. 120.

6 Ibid., p. 153.

7 James Smith and Finis Welch, *Race Differences in Earnings: A Survey of New Evidence* (Santa Monica, Calif.: Rand, 1978), p. 53.

8 Bureau of the Census, *The Social and Economic Status of the Black Population in the United States, 1972.* (Washington, D.C.: U.S. Government Printing Office, 1973), p. 1.

9 Bureau of the Census, *The Social and Economic Status of the Black Population in the United States: An Historical View, 1790–1978* (Washington, D.C.: Government Printing Office, 1978), p. x.

10 Ibid., p. 212.

11 Ibid., p. 60

12 Ibid., p. 61.

13 Ibid., p. 62.

14 Ibid.

15 *The State of Black America 1979* (New York; National Urban League, 1979), p. III.

16 Bureau of the Census, *Social and Economic Status, 1790–1978* p. 61.

17 Diane Wescott and Robert Bednarzik, "Employment and Unemployment: A Report on 1980," *Monthly Labor Review,* February 1981, p. 9.

Notes

18 Bureau of the Census, *Social and Economic Status, 1790–1978*, p. 61.
19 Robert B. Hill, *The Illusion of Black Progress* (Washington: National Urban League, 1978), p. v.
20 Dorothy Newman et al., *Protest, Politics, and Prosperity: Black Americans and White Institutions, 1940–1975* (New York: Pantheon Books, 1978), p. 44.
21 Flournoy A. Coles, Jr., *Black Economic Development* (Chicago: Nelson Hall, 1975), p. 56.

CHAPTER VI

1 E. Franklin Frazier, *Black Bourgeoisie* (New York: Free Press, 1957), pp. 47–53.
2 William Wilson, *The Declining Significance of Race* (Chicago: University of Chicago Press, 1978), p. 129.
3 Ibid., p. 152.
4 Ben J. Wattenberg and Richard Scammon, "Black Progress and Liberal Rhetoric," *Commentary,* April 1973, p. 35.
5 Robert B. Hill, *The Illusion of Black Progress* (Washington, D.C.: National Urban League, 1978), p. 20.
6 Ibid., p. 22.
7 William Brashler, "The Black Middle Class: Making It," *New York Times Magazine,* December 3, 1978, pp. 34ff.
8 Ronald Alsop, "Middle-Class Blacks Worry About Slipping, Still Face Racial Bias," *Wall Street Journal,* November 3, 1980, p. 1.
9 Brashler, "Black Middle Class," p. 34.
10 Alsop, "Middle-Class Blacks Worry," p. 1.
11 James E. Blackwell, *The Black Community: Diversity and Unity* (New York: Dodd, Mead, 1975), pp. 74–88.
12 Bureau of the Census, *The Social and Economic Status of the Black Population in the United States: An Historical View, 1790–1978* (Washington, D.C.: Government Printing Office, 1979), p. 189.
13 Ibid., p. 218.
14 Bureau of the Census, *Social Indicators III* (Washington, D.C.: Government Printing Office, 1980), p. 297.
15 Bureau of the Census, *Social and Economic Status, 1790–1978*, p. 189.
16 Hill, *Illusion of Black Progress*, p. 23.
17 Bureau of the Census, *Social and Economic Status, 1790–1978*, p. 27.
18 Stephen Birmingham, *Certain People: America's Black Elite* (Boston: Little, Brown, 1977), pp. 209–10, 213.

Notes

19 Frazier, *Black Bourgeoisie,* pp. 24–6.
20 Ibid., pp. 208–11.
21 Brashler, "The Black Middle Class," pp. 35–6.
22 Alsop, "Middle-Class Blacks Worry."
23 *New York Times,* December 3, 1978, p. 82.
24 Dorothy Newman et al., *Protest, Politics and Prosperity: Black Americans and White Institutions, 1940–1975* (New York: Pantheon Books, 1978), p. 139.
25 *Twenty Years After Brown: Equal Opportunity in Housing* (Washington, D.C.: U.S. Commission on Civil Rights, 1975), p. 173. Emphasis in original.
26 Frazier, *Black Bourgeoisie,* p. 23.
27 Birmingham, *Certain People,* pp. 24–5.
28 *New York Times,* April 15, 1979, sec. 10, p. 1.
29 Alsop "Middle-Class Blacks Worry," p. 28.
30 *Civil Liberties,* February 1979, p. 8.
31 Frazier, *Black Bourgeoisie,* p. 235.
32 Ibid., p. 236.
33 See Alphonso Pinkney, *Red, Black, and Green: Black Nationalism in the United States* (Cambridge: Cambridge University Press, 1976).
34 Brashler, "Black Middle Class," p. 35.
35 Ibid., p. 155.
36 Alsop, "Middle-Class Blacks Worry," p. 28.
37 Paul Delaney, "Middle-Class Gains Create Tension in Black Community," *New York Times,* February 28, 1978, p. 22.
38 *New York Times,* July 6, 1980, p. E5.
39 *New York Times,* February 27, 1978, p. A4.
40 Jeannye Thornton, "The Quiet Power of America's Black Elite," *U.S. News and World Report,* April 6, 1981, p. 52.
41 *The State of Black America 1979* (Washington, D.C.: National Urban League, 1979), pp. IV–V.
42 *New York Times,* February 26, 1978, p. 1.

CHAPTER VII

1 George Iden, "The Labor Force Experience of Black Youth: A Review," *Monthly Labor Review,* August 1980, p. 11.
2 *New York Times,* March 14, 1979, p. B9.
3 *Wall Street Journal,* February 1, 1979, p. 42.
4 *New York Times,* March 15, 1979, p. A22.
5 Douglas Glasgow, *The Black Underclass: Poverty, Unemployment, and Entrapment of Ghetto Youth* (San Francisco: Jossey-Bass, 1980), p. viii.

Notes

6 *Oakland Tribune/Eastbay Today,* April 7, 1981, p. A6.
7 *New York Times,* March 12, 1979, p. B11.
8 Glasgow, *Black Underclass,* pp. 60, 83.
9 Iden, "Black Youth," p. 10.
10 *New York Times,* March 12, 1979, p. B10.
11 Ibid.
12 *New York Times,* March 11, 1979, p. 44.
13 Bureau of Labor Statistics, *Monthly Labor Review,* October 1979, pp. 11–13.
14 *Wall Street Journal,* February 1, 1979, p. 42.
15 *New York Times,* March 13, 1979, p. B6.
16 Kenneth Clark, "The Role of Race," *New York Times Magazine,* October 5, 1980, pp. 25ff.
17 *Oakland Tribune/Eastbay Today,* May 25, 1981, p. A7.
18 Glasgow, *Black Underclass,* chap. 6.
19 Ibid., pp. 91ff.
20 *New York Times,* February 28, 1978, p. 22.
21 Glasgow, *Black Underclass,* p. 91.
22 Ibid., p. 11.
23 James E. Blackwell, *The Black Community: Diversity and Unity* (New York: Dodd, Mead, 1975), pp. 89–91.
24 Elliot Liebow, *Tally's Corner: A Study of Negro Street Corner Men* (Boston: Little, Brown, 1967).
25 Ibid., p. 57. Emphasis in original.
26 Ibid., p. 211.
27 Claude Brown, *The Children of Ham* (New York: Stein and Day, 1976).
28 Ibid., p. 66
29 Ibid., p. 48.
30 *New York Times,* March 15, 1979, p. A22.

CHAPTER VIII

1 Bureau of the Census, *Statistical Abstract of the United States: 1979* (Washington, D.C.: Government Printing Office, 1979), p. 144.
2 *The State of Black America 1979* (New York: National Urban League, 1979), p. 216.
3 *Oakland Tribune/Eastbay Today,* May 18, 1981, p. B12.
4 *The State of Black America 1979,* p. 97.
5 Ibid., p. 99.
6 *Chronicle of Higher Education,* March 27, 1978, p. 18.
7 Bureau of the Census, *The Social and Economic Status of the*

Notes

Black Population in the United States: An Historical View, 1790–1978 (Washington, D.C.: Government Printing Office, 1978), p. 90.

8 I. F. Stone, "Moving the Constitution to the Back of the Bus," in Nicalous Mills (ed.), *The Great School Bus Controversy* (New York: Teachers College Press, 1973), p. 181.

9 Thomas Sowell, "Are Quotas Good for Blacks?" *Commentary*, June 1978, p. 42.

10 Thomas J. Cottle, *Busing* (Boston: Beacon Press, 1976), p. 2.

11 Ibid., p. 114.

12 Nicalous Mills (ed.), *The Great School Bus Controversy*, p. 6.

13 Ibid., p. 7.

14 Stone, "Moving the Constitution," p. 182.

15 James Coleman, "Integration yes, Busing, NO," *New York Times Magazine*, August 24, 1975, p. 48.

16 United States Commission on Civil Rights, *Fulfilling the Letter and the Spirit of the Law: Desegregation of the Nation's Public Schools* (Washington, D.C.: U.S. Commission on Civil Rights, 1976), p. 312.

17 *It's Not the Distance, It's the Niggers* (New York: NAACP Legal Defense and Educational Fund, 1972), pp. 323–4.

18 Spiro Agnew, "Spiro Agnew on College Admissions," *College Board Review*, Spring 1970.

19 Irving Kristol, "Open Admissions and the Politics of the Absurd," in David Rosen et al. (eds.), *Open Admissions: The Pros and Cons* (Washington, D.C.: Council for Basic Education, 1972), p. 22.

20 Robert Nisbet, "Some Skeptical Observations on Open Admissions," in Rosen et al. (eds.), *Open Admissions: The Pros and Cons*, p. 50.

21 David Rosen, "Open Admissions at the City University of New York: A Case Study," in David Rosen et al. (eds.), *Open Admissions: The Promise and the Lie of Open Access to American Higher Education* (Lincoln, Nebr.: Study Commission on Undergraduate Education and the Education of Teachers, 1973).

22 Quoted in Rosen et al. (eds.), *Open Admissions*, p. 56.

23 Mortimer Smith, "Varieties of Open Admissions," in Rosen et al. (eds.), *Open Admissions: Pros and Cons*, p. 5.

24 Steve Fowler, "Post Secondary Educational Opportunity in Nebraska," in Rosen et al. (eds.), *Open Admissions*, p. 14.

25 Quoted in Seth Brunner, "Post Secondary Educational Opportunity in California," in Rosen et al. (eds.), *Open Admissions*.

26 Ibid., p. 37.

27 Ibid., p. 44.

28 Ibid., p. 52.

29 Rosen, "Open Admissions," in Rosen et al. (eds.), *Open Admissions*, pp. 82–4.
30 Lawrence Podell, *City University Student Survey* (New York: Office of Program and Policy Research, 1977).
31 Ann F. Decker, Ruth Jody, and Felicia Brings, *A Handbook on Open Admissions: Success, Failure, Potential* (Boulder, Colo.: Westview Press, 1976), p. 10.
32 Rosen, "Open Admissions," in Rosen et al. (eds.), *Open Admissions*, pp. 165–6.
33 *Oakland Tribune/Eastbay Today*, March 26, 1981, p. A4.

CHAPTER IX

1 *New York Times*, June 29, 1978, p. A22.
2 *Chronicle of Higher Education*, July 10, 1978, p. 13.
3 Ibid., pp. 11–12.
4 *Chronicle of Higher Education*, June 3, 1978, p. 7.
5 *The Bakke Case, Affirmative Action and Higher Education* (New York: Faculty Action, 1978), p. 20.
6 *New York Times*, November 27, 1977, p. 14.
7 *Higher Education Guidelines: Executive Order 11246* (Washington, D.C.: Department of Health, Education and Welfare, 1972), p. 1.
8 Ibid., pp. 2–3.
9 Ibid., p. 3.
10 John E. Flemming, Gerald R. Gill, and David H. Swinton, *The Case for Affirmative Action for Blacks in Higher Education* (Washington, D.C.: Howard University Press, 1978), p. 7.
11 Ibid., pp. 70–4.
12 "After Bakke," *Rights*, September/October 1978.
13 These data were compiled by the American Civil Liberties Union, New York, June 14, 1977.
14 *New York Times*, September 20, 1977, p. 34.
15 Ibid.
16 Ibid.
17 *Chronicle of Higher Education*, July 3, 1978, p. 12.
18 *Chronicle of Higher Education*, July 10, 1978, p. 13.
19 *Guardian*, August 16, 1976, p. 8.
20 Steven Roberts, "The Bakke Case Moves to the Factory," *New York Times Magazine*, February 25, 1979, p. 84.
21 *New York Times*, March 29, 1979, p. A19.
22 *New York Times*, June 28, 1979, p. B12.
23 Ibid.

Notes

24 *New York Times Magazine*, February 25, 1979, p. 101.
25 Ibid.
26 John Flemming et al., *Case for Affirmative Action*, p. 90.

CHAPTER X

1 See, for example, C. Vann Woodward, *The Strange Career of Jim Crow* (New York: Oxford University Press, 1957); and C. Vann Woodward, *Reunion and Reaction* (New York: Doubleday, 1956).
2 Michael W. Miles, *The Odyssey of the American Right* (New York: Oxford University Press, 1980), pp. 318–19.
3 Ibid., pp. 319–20.
4 *New York Times*, June 3, 1981, p. D8.
5 *New York Times*, December 3, 1983, pp. 1, 12.
6 Alan Crawford, *Thunder on the Right: The New Right and the Politics of Resentment* (New York: Pantheon Books, 1980), p. 256.
7 *New York Times*, October 30, 1960, p. A16.
8 *Oakland Tribune/Eastbay Today*, April 25, 1981, p. A4.
9 *Parade*, February 15, 1981, p. 20.
10 Ronald V. Dellums, "Socialism for the Rich or Help for the Needy?" *Oakland Tribune/Eastbay Today*, April 13, 1981, p. A9.
11 *Oakland Tribune/Eastbay Today*, May 25, 1981, p. A7.
12 *New York Times*, June 2, 1981, p. 1.
13 Crawford, *Thunder on the Right*, p. 259.

INDEX

Index

Index

Index

PACE UNIVERSITY LIBRARY

New York, NY   10038